Academic and Research Writing

Essential Skills and Styles

Academic and Research Writing

Essential Skills and Styles

Sanjay Kumar Dutta

Lecturer, Department of English,
Vyasanagar Autonomous College,
Jajpur, Odisha

New Century Publications
New Delhi, India

NEW CENTURY PUBLICATIONS
4800 / 24, Bharat Ram Road,
Ansari Road, Daryaganj,
New Delhi - 110 002 (India)

Tel.: 011-2324 7798, 4358 7398, 4101 7798
E-mail: info@newcenturypublications.com • indiatax@vsnl.com
www.newcenturypublications.com

Editorial office:
LG – 7, Aakarshan Bhawan,
4754-57/23, Ansari Road, Daryaganj,
New Delhi – 110 002

Tel.: 011-4356 0919

First Published: **2018**

ISBN: **978-81-7708-471-9**

Published by New Century Publications and printed at Milan Enterprises, New Delhi.

Designs: Patch Creative Unit, New Delhi.

PRINTED IN INDIA

About the Book

Writing good English is important in many contexts of our lives. Mastering writing skills can make us excel in both academic and professional levels. Students with good writing skills have an edge over others as they can effectively convey what they have learnt. English is used for a variety of purposes, namely writing books, research papers, dissertations, term-papers, book reviews, press statements, company reports, essays, letters and other writings of professional and non-professional nature. Moreover, the use of English as a business language is widespread in India.

This book is meant for a cross-section of learners and users of English language, viz. students, teachers, authors, reviewers, journalists, business executives and others interested in acquiring and improving English language skills.

The book provides step-by-step guidance and explains all the concepts and rules of the language in simple and easily comprehensible terms. Besides simplified explanations and helpful illustrations, the book provides information which every user of English language needs to convey his/her ideas and views in grammatically correct sentences.

If you think of English language as a toolbox for life, then this book contains many useful tools for your learning. Whether you are writing a business e-mail or a research paper, the present work will assist you in becoming a better writer in English.

In short, this book is a rich resource for anyone who needs to communicate in English effectively.

About the Author

Dr. Sanjay Kumar Dutta is currently Lecturer in the Department of English, Vyasanagar Autonomous College, Jajpur, Odisha. His areas of specialization include English language and literature. He had earlier taught at Orissa Engineering College, Bhubaneswar. He has authored a book titled *Essential Skills for Social and Professional Success* and also published research papers on contemporary literature in various national and international journals.

Dr. Dutta has attended and presented papers at various national and international seminars/conferences. He is also a member of the Odisha Association for English Studies.

Contents

Preface

Writing is a very important part of our academic life. We write assignments that may range from one paragraph to several pages. Writing is about communicating with words and academic writing is a specialized form of communication that aims at a more specific audience. It is about choosing words carefully to communicate complex ideas to a range of readers and audiences. Such writing reflects the voices and practices of scholarly communities that are dedicated to the pursuit of knowledge. Academic writing is always a form of evaluation that asks you to demonstrate knowledge and show proficiency with certain disciplinary skills of thinking, interpreting, and presenting. Your success with academic writing is predicated on how well you understand what you are doing as you write and then how you approach the writing task. Effective writing skills are essential not only for attaining professional credentials but also for advancement in one's career.

There are many different genres of writing, including poetry, short-story writing, and formal legal English and business writing. These different styles of writing have their own characteristics. In much the same way, academic writing is a particular genre, with its own distinctive style, forms of expression and vocabulary. The skills of academic writing can be learnt, and anyone who wants to improve their academic writing can acquire such skills.

Academic writing needs to be very clear and precise. In a research context, the student is writing about fairly complex ideas and these have to be expressed with great precision. Moreover, in research, it is frequently the case that one idea follows from another or that when analyzing the data, one procedure follows another. Academic writing thus needs to proceed very logically and systematically, describing first one process, then explaining how this relates to the next issue, and then describing the second process. Good academic writing makes clear the linkages between different aspects of the subject being described or analyzed.

Mastering writing skills can make us excel at both academic and professional level. Students with good writing skills have an edge over others as they can effectively convey what they have learnt. English is used for a variety of purposes, namely, writing books, research papers, dissertations, term papers, book reviews, press statements, company reports, essays, letters and other writings of professional and non-professional nature.

This book is an attempt to provide a step-by-step guidance to understand the concepts and rules of the English language. Besides simplified explanations and helpful illustrations, the book provides information which every user of English language needs to convey his/her ideas and views in grammatically correct sentences.

Acknowledgements

I would like to place on record my sincere thanks to my friend Dr. Sambit Kumar Panigrahi of Ravenshaw University for his gracious assistance in going through all the chapters and suggesting necessary changes in refining the manuscript. Thanks are also due to my friends Chinmaya, Soumya, Jagabandhu, and Narendra for their constant inspiration and encouragement.

I express my gratitude to the principal and colleagues at Vyasanagar Autonomous College for encouraging and supporting my academic efforts.

I am indebted to my wife Kunmun and son Atish for bearing with me during the preparation of this book.

Finally, use of information, for a few texts and examples, from various websites is thankfully acknowledged.

Jajpur **Sanjay Kumar Dutta**

1

Basics of Academic and Research Writing

1.1 Why Do We Write?

We write to learn, to share our learning with others, to express our creativity, to accomplish our work and the work of others, and to connect ideas and people. It is the primary basis upon which our work, learning and intellect is judged in colleges; in the work place and in the community. It is the vehicle by which our ideas and feelings are articulated and expressed. Good writing skills are essential for successful performance in any academic discipline and profession. Mastering writing skills can help us in excelling both at the academic and professional level. Students with good writing skills have an edge over others as they effectively convey what they have learnt.

All writing texts that we produce can be categorized as academic and non-academic. Non-academic writing is generally employed in personal letters, newspaper reports, literary writings, and internet postings. Whereas, academic writing is a kind of writing that we undertake for our academic pursuits. These, in turn, help us to grow in our professional life. The most common types of academic writings are essays, dissertations, and research papers. The ability to write well in English is the result of hard work and constant practice. So, it is essential that students should be aware of what academic writing is and how it could be developed.

1.2 What is Academic Writing?

Writing is a very important part of our academic life in schools and colleges. We have to write assignments that may range from one paragraph to several pages. Academic writing is formal and needs particular care to be organized in a certain way. Academic writing in English is probably different from academic writing in our native language.

Academic writing is a specialized form of communication that aims at a more specific audience. It is about choosing words carefully to communicate complex ideas to a range of readers and audiences. Such writing reflects the voices and practices of scholarly communities that are dedicated to the pursuit of knowledge. Academic writing is always a form of evaluation that asks you to demonstrate knowledge and show proficiency with certain disciplinary skills of thinking, interpreting, and presenting. Your success with academic writing is predicated on how well you understand what you are doing as you write and then how you approach the writing task. Effective writing skills are essential not only for attaining professional credentials but also for advancement in one's career.

Academic writing is one of the cornerstones of our university study. In all disciplines, students need writing to express their ideas clearly. It goes without saying that clarity in thought and expression depends on the students' understanding of the course content.

Academic writing is distinctly different from other forms of writing. Though on the surface, it may appear to have similarities with other forms of writing, it is different in every aspect—from purpose to tone, from structure to style, and in word choice.

Although sometimes treated synonymously, academic and scholarly writings do have some variations in their purposes and characteristics. Academic and scholarly writings bear striking resemblances with each other. However, subtle differences do exist between the two. While academic writing may be defined broadly as any writing completed to fulfil university or college requirements, scholarly writing is initiated to inform a specialized audience in a particular field. Scholarly writing is crafted by one professional for other professionals. Graduate students may wish to think of scholarly writing as a subset of academic writing. The purpose of academic writing is to present information about a specific subject precisely and objectively.

The purpose of scholarly writing is the advancement of knowledge within a specific field. More than a demonstration of the author's expertise, scholarly writing is produced to add to the body of knowledge, extending, challenging, or expanding what is known or believed within the field. Thus, while all scholarly writings are academic writings, not all academic writings are scholarly writings.

1.3 Academic Writing as a Genre

There are many different genres of writing, including poetry, short-story writing, and formal legal English and business writing. These different styles of writing have their own characteristics. In much the same way, academic writing is a particular genre, with its own distinctive style, forms of expression and vocabulary. The skills of academic writing can be learnt, and anyone who wants to improve his/her academic writing can acquire such skills.

Academic writing needs to be very clear and precise. In a research context, the student writes about fairly complex ideas and these have to be expressed with great precision. Moreover, in research, it is frequently the case that one idea follows from another or that when analyzing the data, one procedure follows another. Academic writing thus needs to proceed very logically and systematically, describing first, one process, then explaining how this relates to the next issue, and then describing the second process. Good academic writing makes clear the linkages between the different aspects of the subject being described or analyzed.

1.4 Academic versus Non-academic Writing

There is a considerable point of difference between academic and non-academic writing. Both varieties of writing are different in many ways—in context, in style, in organization, grammar and vocabulary. The other aspects in which academic and non-academic writings can be contrasted are as under:

- Academic writing is formal while non-academic writing tends to be personal.
- Academic writing is based on facts and therefore factual, whereas non-academic writing is based on our own point of view.
- Academic writing focuses on a specific field or category, but non-academic writing might be a general issue.
- Academic writing is more rigid and logical while non-academic writing is free style writing.
- Academic readers need some prior knowledge of the topic while targeted readers of non-academic writing are a more general group with everyday knowledge.

1.5 Purpose of Academic Writing

We should be clear about why we are writing. The most common purposes for which we write include the following:

- To report on a piece of research we have conducted.
- To answer a question posed to us.
- To discuss a subject of common interest and give our views.
- To synthesize research done by others on a topic.

In general, academic writing is found in essays, course papers, research papers, books, reports, translations, theses, dissertations, articles, technical reports, critiques, and abstracts.

1.6 Features of Academic Writing

Written English, like spoken English, may be formal or informal. As there are no fixed rules for the layout of an academic work, the following features may apply to most of the forms of academic writing. These are as follows:

- It is mostly formal, impersonal and objective.
- It has a rational tone.
- It uses impersonal pronouns, phrases, and passive forms of verbs.
- Most of these writings include references to other writings.
- It has a clear and logical organization.

- It uses simple and longer sentences.
- It uses formal vocabulary appropriate for particular academic context.
- The structure of the writing varies according to the particular type of writing.

Other distinctive features will depend upon the specific types of academic writing.

1.7 Language of Academic Writing

Academic writing is an area that is affected significantly by limited English proficiency. While oral skills can be developed as students engage in meaningful activities, skills in writing must be explicitly taught. The writing process, which involves planning, drafting, editing, and revising written work, allows students to express their ideas at their level of proficiency with teacher (or peer) guidance and explicit corrective feedback. However, for English learners, it is critical that a lot of meaningful discussion takes place prior to asking students to write because such dialogues help connect ideas in support of writing. Writing is also facilitated by such things as teacher modelling, posting of writing samples, providing sentence frames, and even having students copy words or text until they gain more independent proficiency. This kind of constant exposure to words and sentence patterning allows them to become familiar with the conventions of how words and sentences are put together in the language.

English learners should be encouraged to write in English early, especially if they have skills in their native language, and should be provided frequent opportunities to express their ideas in writing. Errors in writing are expected and should be viewed as part of the natural process of language acquisition. Providing scaffolded writing tools, such as partially completed graphic organizers for pre-writing and sentence frames for organizing key points and supporting details will help students.

Graduate students and professionals must be aware of the

level of formality required in the works they produce. Generally, authors employ one of the three basic levels of language: formal, semi-formal, and informal. The level of language for any work should be based on the target audience and the purpose of the work.

Informal language is rarely used in academic or scholarly writing. This level is more conversational in style, often does not follow conventional rules of grammar and mechanics, and may include the use of slangs. Personal letters, conversations, social networking entries, and dialogue in popular forms of literature are usually written in informal English.

In academic writing, authors may use either semi-formal or formal language. The choice should be based on audience and purpose. Authors use semi-formal language in business letters to individuals well-known to them. Conventional rules of grammar and mechanics apply. However, the tone is more personal. Authors refer to themselves in the first person (i.e. I, we) and to their readers in second person (i.e., you). Judicious use of contractions, shorter sentences, and more reader-friendly vocabulary mark this level.

Formal language is generally used in academic and scholarly writing. Conventional rules of grammar and mechanics apply. However, the tone is more serious. Authors use third person in referring to themselves and to their readers. Contractions are not used. Sentences may be more complex in structure. Vocabulary is more formal and precise. Abbreviations and acronyms are used judiciously. Since the audience is often other people in the same profession, authors may use more technical terms. People within the profession know and understand these terms and expect them to be used. However, if the audience is more general, including people not familiar with the vocabulary of the profession, the use of technical terms should be kept to the minimum. Authors should also consider defining the technical terms that are used.

Certain words which we frequently encounter in everyday communication may not be suitable for use in academic writing. These include words which are casual (informal) and commonly used only in spoken English such as *kids* and *boss* for which the Standard English is *children* and *manager*. This does not mean that informal language is inferior to the formal language. It simply means that there are words which are more appropriate than others for use in each context. Table 1.1 provides examples of casual (informal) words and their academic counterparts.

Table 1.1: Casual (Informal) Words and Their Alternative Academic Words

Casual (informal) words	Academic words
Worry	Concern
Story	Account
Get rid of	Eradicate
A lot of	Considerable
Not enough	Insufficient
Trouble	Difficulty
Big	Significant
Way (of doing)	Method
Bring things together	Synthesize
Thing	Object
Not much research	Little research
Not many studies	Little studies

1.8 Academic Style

In the broadest sense, *style* is the total of all the choices a writer makes concerning words and their arrangements. In this sense, style may be good or bad—good if the choices are appropriate to the writer's purpose, bad if they are not. More narrowly, style has a positive, approving sense, as when we say that someone has a style. There are no rules for academic style that apply to all situations. However, there are a few guidelines that should help us develop a style of our own. The principal characteristics of written academic style are listed below.

1.8.1 Evidence-based: Perhaps the most important distinguishing feature of written academic style is that it is evidence-based. Writers support their arguments and claims with evidence from the body of knowledge relevant to their discipline.

1.8.2 Words of Classical Origin: Unlike everyday English, academic writing is characterized by a high frequency of words of classical origin (Greek and Latin). The main reason for this is that Latin was the *lingua academica* during the European renaissance. In other words, it was the international language of scholars. Even until relatively recently, great works of science, such as Isaac Newton's *Philosophiæ Naturalis Principia Mathematica* (1687), were written in Latin. Even where academic texts were written in English, words of classical origin were used for concepts and phenomena for which there was no equivalent in English.

1.8.3 Impersonal: In the interest of objectivity, academic writers tend to remove themselves from the writing. The focus is on *what* happened, *how* it was done and *what* was found. The *who* (the writer) is not normally given very much attention. This is one of the reasons why personal pronouns (I and we) tend not to be used. In addition, academic texts rarely address the reader directly and the pronoun normally used for this, *you*, is avoided.

1.8.4 Contracted Forms Avoided: Contracted forms (e.g. it's, don't, isn't, aren't) should not be used in academic writing. The only exception would be if you are transcribing a recorded conversation or an interview.

1.8.5 Precise and Detailed: One of the most noticeable features of an academic writing is that it is very precise and detailed. This relates to the setting out and development of the thinking and the ideas as well as to the language used in the writing. Conclusions should use tentative language. Avoid absolute statements such as *unemployment causes crime*. Instead use cautious phrases: *unemployment may cause crime* or *tends to cause crime*.

Avoid repetition and redundancy. Repetition means repeating a word instead of using a synonym to provide variety, which makes the text more interesting. Thus,

Instead of: Most family businesses employ less than ten people. These businesses...

Use: Most family businesses employ less than ten people. These firms...

Redundancy, i.e. repeating an idea or including an irrelevant point, suggests that the writer is not fully in control of the material. It gives the impression that the writer does not properly understand the language. Avoid phrases such as:

Homelessness is a global problem in the whole world.

Use: Homelessness is a global problem.

In short, good writing involves the following:

- Clear connection of ideas.
- An academic style.
- Correctly organized sentences and paragraphs.
- Avoidance of common mistakes.
- Proper presentation of writing.

1.9 Vocabulary Development

Cambridge Advanced Learner's Dictionary defines vocabulary as all the words a particular individual knows and uses, and all the words that exist in a particular language or subject. Vocabulary is considered the key to communication and plays a great role for learners in acquiring a language. It is the single most important area of language competence and is of concern to all language skills. Students sometimes face a lot of difficulty in choosing a proper word to describe things. This is because we have a limited number of words in our mind.

As we study, we will hear and read a lot of new words, some of which are general academic words while others are specific to our subject or more technical. Both types of words are important for developing the vocabulary. Here are some tips to learn new words and use them effectively in speaking and writing.

- Keep an English language dictionary close by to find the meaning of words you are doubtful about.
- Preferably use an English-English dictionary.
- Oxford Advanced Learner's Dictionary is especially useful.
- Use a thesaurus to build your knowledge of synonyms and antonyms.
- Use your academic reading to develop the vocabulary you need in your discipline.

2

Word Formation

The store of words is by no means fixed for ever. It is enlarged by the process which can be either linguistic or non-linguistic. Also, new words may be introduced into a language by borrowing or by coinage. There are a number of processes which help in producing new words in English according to the requirement of the user. The major sources of word formation in English are as under:

- Using prefixes and suffixes.
- Borrowing.
- Blending.
- Compounding.
- Clipping.

2.1 Using Prefixes and Suffixes

One of the ways in which new words are created is by adding suffixes and prefixes. Prefixes and suffixes are set of letters that are added to the beginning or end of another word. They are not words in their own right and cannot stand on their own in a sentence. Some prefixes and suffixes are part of our living language, in the sense that we regularly use them to create new words. Prefixes and suffixes are added to an existing word in order to create a new word with a different meaning. The addition of a suffix often changes a word from one class to another.

2.1.2 Why Do We Learn Prefixes and Suffixes? Prefixes and suffixes add meaning to thousands of words. Learn a few prefixes and suffixes, and you open up the meaning of thousands of words. Tables 2.1 and 2.2 contain examples which will certainly help students to build up their vocabulary.

Table 2.1: Prefixes with Meaning and Examples

Prefixes	Meaning	Examples
ab/abs	away from	abnormal, abscond, absent
ad	to	adhere, adjoin, advance, adjacent
Ante	before	antecedent, antedate
anthropos	man	anthropology, misanthropy
anti	against	antifreeze, antisocial, antibiotic
Aqua	water	aquarium
Arch	chief	archbishop, archtype
Auto	self	autobiography, autocrat
bi, bis	two	bicycle, biannual, biennia
Cent	hundred	centenary, century
centi	one hundredth	centigrade, centimetre
centri	of the middle	centrifugal, eccentric
Chromos	time	chronology, chronic
circum, cir	around	circumscribe, circle
co	with	coexist, coordinate
com, con, co, col	with, together	combine, contact, collect, co-worker
de	away from, down	depart, decline
dia	across	diagonal, diameter
En	to put into	endanger, enslave
epi	upon, at	epidemic
ex	former	ex- student, ex-president
extra	outside	extramarital, extraordinary
Fore	before	foreground, forehead, foretell
Hyper	over/above	hypersensitive, hypertension
il	not	illiterate, illogical
inter	between, among	international, interpose
Intra	within	intravenous
mal, male	bad, ill, wrong	malpractice, malfunction
Maxi	very large	maximum
meta	change	metaphor, metamorphosis
micro	small	microwave, microscopic
milli	thousand	milligram, millionaire
Mini	little	miniature, minibus

Mis	wrong, badly	mistreat, mistake, misplace
Mono	one, single	monologue, monotonous
Mono	one, alone, single	monopoly, monotone, monologue, monosyllable
multi	many	multi-national, multi-purpose
Neo	new	neoclassical
non	not, the reverse of	nonsense, non-profit
non	not	non-resident, nonsense
omni	everywhere, all	omnipresent, omnipotent
Over	too much	overtired, overeat, overdo
Pan	all, worldwide	panorama, pan-American
Para	beyond	paramilitary, paradox
Per	through	pervade, perceive
Poly	many	polysyllable, polygon
post	after	postpone, post-mortem
Pre	before, earlier	preview, prehistoric, preface
pro	for, in favour of	pro-Indian, pro-communist
pseudo	false	pseudo-intellectual
Re	again, back	reread, replace, rewind
Re	again, back	retell, recall, recede
semi	half	semicircular, semi-final
sub	under	subway, submarine
Sub	under, less	submarine, subway , subliminal
Super	over, above	superstar, superimpose
Supra	above	suprasensuous
Trans	across	transcontinental, transverse
Un	not	uninterested, unhelpful, unethical
un, uni	one	unidirectional, unanimous, unilateral
Under	below	underground, undercoat
Uni	one	uniform, unitary
vice	deputy	vice-principal, vice-chancellor

Table 2.2: Suffixes with Meaning and Examples

Suffixes	Meaning	Examples
able, ible, ble	able to	edible, saleable
Ful	full of	fearful
Ism	the practice of, support of	patriotism
ity, ty, y	the state of, character of	unity, shifty, showy
Ive	having the nature of	active
Less	lacking, without	heartless
Logy	the study of	biology
Ment	the act of, the state of	retirement
Ness	the quality of	eagerness
ship	the art or skill of, the ability to	leadership
Some	full of, like	troublesome
Ist	one who makes, does	artist
ant, ent, er, or	one who	occupant, respondent, teacher, creator

2.2 Borrowings

It is the process of obtaining words from another language. English language is full of foreign origin and accommodating enough to accept words from various languages. It has taken many expressions from the ancient languages particularly, words from Latin, French, and Greek. These borrowings usually have academic and literary associations. Table 2.3 which contains words with their English meaning will help students to build their vocabulary.

Table 2.3: English Words from Other Languages

Word	Root	Meaning
ad hoc	Latin	for a particular purpose
ad infinitum	Latin	for ever, endlessly
ad interim	Latin	for the time being
alma mater	Latin	fostering mother; used by students to their school
avant garde	French	modern in comparison to the period in

		which they happen
Bonafide	Latin	genuine, real
Chauffeur	French	person whose job is to drive a car
corrigendum	Latin	correction made
Crèche	French	child care
Cuisine	French	kind of cooking product
de facto	Latin	in reality
e.g.	Latin	for example, such as
en bloc	French	together
en masse	French	all together
en route	French	on the way
Errata	Latin	errors
etc.	Latin	and so on
ex officio	Latin	by virtue of his office
ex tempore	Latin	without preparation
Fiasco	Italian	total failure
ibid.	Latin	in the same place
in absentia	Latin	while not present
Incognito	Italian	in disguise
inter alia	Latin	among other things
lingua franca	Italian	a common language
magnum opus	Latin	masterpiece of an artist
mala fide	Latin	in bad faith
modus operandi	Latin	a method of doing something
nota bene (n.b.)	Latin	note well
op. cit.	Latin	in the work mentioned before
par excellence	French	extra excellence
per annum	Latin	annually
per capita	Latin	per person
per cent	Latin	per hundred
post mortem	Latin	medical examination after death
pro forma	Latin	for the sake of
sine die	Latin	indefinitely
status quo	Latin	as before
vice versa	Latin	the order being reversed
vis-à-vis	French	regarding, about
viva voce	Latin	oral examination
viz.	Latin	namely

2.3 Compounding

A compounding is a union of two or more words to convey a unit idea or special meaning that is not as clearly or quickly conveyed by separated words. It is one of the most productive word formation processes in English. Compound words have three written forms: hyphenated, written open (as separate words), or written solid (closed).

2.3.1 Hyphenated Compound: Also called a unit modifier, it is simply a combination of words joined by a hyphen or hyphens. The hyphen is a mark of punctuation that not only unites but separates the component words. Thus, it aids in understanding and readability and ensures correct pronunciation.

2.3.2 Open Compound: It is a combination of words so closely associated that they convey the idea of a single concept but are spelled as unconnected words.

The following rules can help the students to form compound words correctly.

Rule 1: Certain expressions are written as separate words when they are used as noun phrases but are hyphenated or written solid when they are used as adjectives before nouns.

Examples:

Deep sea..deep-sea fauna
Deep water.....................................deep-water technology
Food web.......................................food-web dependencies
Dark green...dark-green algae

Rule 2: When verbs are combined with a preposition or adverb, write them as two words. When the same two words are used as nouns or adjectives, they should be hyphenated or joined.

Examples:

Break up...break-up
Build up..build-up
Run off ....run-off
Shut down..shut-down
Shut in...shut-in

Rule 3: When two nouns are joined, do not put hyphen or separate them.

Examples: housewife, housework, schoolboy, milkman, chairman, postmaster, classroom, bedroom, timetable, workshop, teatime, homework, roommate etc.

Rule 4: When a determiner is combined with a noun or pronoun, make it a close compound.

Examples: anyone, anybody, anything, someone, sometimes, somebody etc.

Rule 4: When a noun or an adjective is combined with word in "ing" form, normally it is hyphenated.

Examples: letter-writing, story-telling, family-planning, money-making, walking-stick, waiting-room, dining-room, swimming-pool, drinking-water, easy-going, long-standing, etc.

Rule 5: When a noun, an adjective or an adverb is combined with an "ed" word, it is hyphenated.

Examples: home-made, air-conditioned, hand-made, self-centred, bald-headed, middle-aged, short-sleeved, ready-made, well-dressed, well-known, well-behaved etc.

2.4 Blending

It is a popular word formation process. It involves taking two or more words, removing parts of each and joining the residues together to create a new word whose form and meaning are taken from the source words. The fundamental characteristic of a blend is that it cannot be broken into meaningful parts. If it is so, it is not a blend but a compound. Following are the examples of blend words:

Blog: web + log
Breathalyser: breath + analyser
Bromance: brother + romance
Brunch: breakfast + lunch
Cartune: cartoon + tune
Chunnel: channel + tunnel
Dramality: drama + reality
Eurasia: Europe + Asia

Foodoholic: food + alcoholic
Frenemy: friend + enemy
Girus: giant + virus
Glimmer: gleam + slimmer
Globish: global + English
Glocal: global + local
Guesstimate: guess + estimate
Heliport: helicopter + airport
Internet: international + network
Mocktail: mock + cocktail
Motel: motor + hotel
Sexport: sex + export
Slanguage: slang + language
Smog: smoke + fog
Spanglish: Spanish + English
Spork: spoon + fork

2.5 Clipping

It is a process of word formation by dropping a significant portion of an existing word in order to find only a base word to be used freely. It is a kind of abbreviation of a word in which one part is 'clipped' off the rest and remaining word means essentially the same thing as what the whole word meant. It is a process of reducing a word to one of its parts. Though clipping sometimes does not form a part of a standard lexicon of a language, they originate as a terminology of a special group in the familiarity of a milieu where a hint is sufficient to indicate the whole.

Though, there are different types of clipping, only the following types are commonly used in English.

2.5.1 Back Clipping: This is the most common type of all. There is a dropping or omission of a letter or syllable from the end of a longer word. The beginning of the word is retained and the end of the word is clipped.

Examples:

Ad: advertisement

Demo: demonstration
Doc: doctor
Exam: examination
Feb: February
Gas: gasoline
Gym: gymnasium
Lab: laboratory
Math: mathematics
Memo: memorandum
Mike: microphone
Pub: public house

2.5.2 Fore-clipping: In fore-clipping, omission of letters takes place at the beginning of a word and the final part of a word is retained.

Examples:

Bike: motor bike
Chute: parachute
Phone: telephone
Round: around
Varsity: university

3

Commonly Confused Words

Words that sound alike or look alike (moral/morale) often confuse students.

3.1 Commonly Confused Words with Meaning

The following list of commonly confused words with simple definitions will help students decide which spelling fits their sentences.

Accept: to receive.
Except: with the exclusion of.

Allude: to make indirect reference to.
Elude: to avoid.

Allusion: indirect reference.
Illusion: false idea, misleading appearance.

Already: by this time.
All ready: fully prepared.

Altogether: thoroughly.
All together: everyone/everything in one place.

Aloud: out loud.
Allowed: permitted.

Altar: a sacred table in a church.
Alter: to change.

Amoral: not concerned with right or wrong.
Immoral: not following accepted moral standards.

Appraise: to assess.
Apprise: to inform someone.

Assent: agreement, approval.
Ascent: the action of rising or climbing up.

Aural: relating to the ears or hearing.
Oral: relating to the mouth; spoken.

Beside: close to; next to.
Besides: except for; in addition.

Born: brought into life.
Borne: past participle of "to bear" (carry).

Breath: air taken in (noun).
Breathe: to take in air (verb).

Brake: device for stopping.
Break: destroy; make into pieces.

Bare: naked; to uncover.
Bear: to carry; to put up with.

Bated: in phrase *with bated breath,* i.e. in great suspense.
Baited: with bait attached or inserted.

Bazaar: A Middle Eastern market.
Bizarre: strange.

Berth: a bunk in a ship, train etc.
Birth: the emergence of a baby from the womb.

Breach: to break through, or break a rule; a gap.
Breech: the back part of a gun barrel.

Broach: to raise a subject for discussion.
Brooch: a piece of jewellery.

Canvas: heavy cloth.
Canvass: to take a survey.

Capital: major city.
Capitol: government building.

Complement: something that completes.
Compliment: praise, flattery.

Council: governing body.
Counsel: advice; to give advice.

Censure: to criticize strongly.
Censor: to ban parts of a book or film; a person who does this.

Cereal: a grass producing an edible grain.
Serial: happening in a series.

Chord: a group of musical notes.
Cord: a length of string.

Climactic: forming a climax.
Climatic: relating to climate.

Coarse: rough.
Course: a direction; a school subject; part of a meal.

Complacent: smug and self-satisfied.
Complaisant: willing to please.

Cue: a signal for action; a wooden rod.
Queue: a line of people or vehicles.

Curb: to keep something in check; a control or limit.
Kerb: (in British English) the stone edge of a pavement.

Currant: a dried grape.
Current: happening now; a flow of water, air, or electricity.

Disinterested: impartial.
Uninterested: not interested.

Draught: a current of air.
Draft: a first version of a piece of writing.

Draw: an even score at the end of a game.
Drawer: a sliding storage compartment.

Dual: having two parts.
Duel: a fight or contest between two people.

Dessert: final, sweet course in a meal.
Desert: to abandon; dry, sandy area.

Discreet: modest, prudent behaviour.
Discrete: a separate thing, distinct.

Everyday: routine, commonplace, ordinary (adj.).
Every day: each day, succession (adj. + noun).

Forth: forward.
Fourth: number four in a list.

Human: relating to the species homo sapiens.
Humane: compassionate.

Its: possessive form of "it".
It's: contraction for "it is".

Later: after a time.
Latter: second one of two things.

Lightning: storm-related electricity.
Lightening: making lighter.

Maybe: perhaps (adv.).
May be: might be (verb).

Moral: distinguishing right from wrong; lesson of a story.
Morale: attitude or outlook usually of a group.

Personal: intimate; owned by a person.
Personnel: employees.

Rational: having reason or understanding.
Rationale: principles of opinion, beliefs.

Raise: to lift up.
Raze: to tear down.

3.2 Indian and Standard English Words

Some examples are given in Table 3.1.

Table 3.1: Indian and Standard English Words

Indian	Standard English
Allopathy	Western medicine
Almirah	Cupboard
Baggage	Luggage
Banian	Vest
Bogie	Coach
Canteen	Cafeteria
Cheater	Cheat
Compounder	Dispenser
Cooker	Cook
Cost	Price

Cover	Envelop
Dustbin	Waste basket
Footpath	Pavement
Freshers	First timers, freshmen
Full pant	Trouser
Good name	First name
Hotel	Restaurant
Latrine	Lavatory
Mess	Hostel
Pencil cutter	Sharpener
Peon	Office attendant
Petrol pump	Gas station
Pin code	Area code/zip code
Purse	Wallet
Tariff	Charges
Visiting card	Business card

4

Synonyms and Antonyms

Synonyms are words whose meanings are similar, but not exactly the same. Antonyms are opposites of the word. They are of great help in choosing the right word for the right use. But their use is determined by the context. So, one should be cautious in choosing the right words for the right situations to avoid repetition. They have certain common grounds within which they are interchangeable; but outside of that each has its own special province, within which any other word comes as an intruder. To write or speak to the best of purpose, one should know in the first place all the words from which he/she may choose, and then the exact reason why in any case any particular word should be chosen.

However, knowing these antonyms and synonyms will help us in using the correct expression suitable for our purpose of writing and conveying the intended meaning. Therefore, a detailed list of synonyms and antonyms is given in Table 4.1 to enrich the writer's vocabulary.

Table 4.1: List of Synonyms and Antonyms

Word	Synonym	Antonym
abandon	desert, forsake	keep, continue, support
abbreviate	shorten, condense	lengthen, increase
ability	skill, aptitude	incompetence, inability
able	capable, qualified	incapable, incompetent
above	overhead, high, aloft	below
abundant	ample, sufficient	scanty, insufficient
accurate	correct, right	wrong, inaccurate
achieve	accomplish, attain	fail, miss
active	energetic, lively	lethargic, idle, sluggish
adamant	firm, unyielding	manoeuvrable, yielding

add	increase, total	subtract, take away
adequate	sufficient, enough	insufficient, sparse
adjourn	postpone, recess	recommence, continue
adult	grown-up, mature	child, immature
advocate	support, recommend	oppose, deprecate
after	following, next	before
afraid	frightened, scared	courageous, brave
aggressive	assertive, pushy	passive, peaceful
aid	help, assist	hinder, obstruct
always	ever, endlessly	never
amateur	beginner, novice	professional
ambitious	aspiring, driven	lazy, indifferent
antagonize	provoke, embitter	soothe, tranquilize
apparent	obvious, evident	hidden, obscure
approve	accept, ratify, endorse	disapprove, censure
arrive	reach, come	depart, leave
arrogant	haughty, stuck-up	humble, modest
artificial	fake, synthetic	real, authentic
atrocious	dreadful, contemptible	kind, wonderful
authentic	genuine, real, factual	false, artificial
average	ordinary, fair	unusual, exceptional
awful	dreadful, atrocious	pleasant, wonderful
awkward	clumsy, uncoordinated	graceful, comfortable
ban	prohibit, forbid, outlaw	allow, permit
barren	unproductive, infertile	fertile, productive
bashful	shy, timid	outgoing, assured
beautiful	graceful, attractive	ugly, hideous
before	prior, earlier	after, behind
beginning	start, initiate	finish, end
believe	trust, accept	doubt, distrust
below	under, lower	above
beneficial	useful, advantageous	harmful, adverse
best	finest, incomparable	worst
birth	Beginning	death, end
blend	combine, mix	separate
bottom	base, foundation	top
brave	courageous, bold, heroic	cowardly, timid
break	fracture, burst	repair, heal

brief	short, concise	long
broad	wide, expansive	narrow
busy	active, occupied	idle, inactive
buy	Purchase	sell
calm	quiet, tranquil, still	excited, turbulent
capture	apprehends, seize, arrest	free, release
care	concern, protection	neglect
careful	cautious, watchful	careless, reckless
cease	stop, discontinue	continue, recommence
certain	positive, sure, definite	uncertain, unsure
charming	delightful, appealing	obnoxious, gross, vulgar
chilly	cool, nippy	warm
chubby	plump, podgy	thin, skinny
clarify	explain, simplify	confuse
close	shut, fasten	open
close	near, imminent	far
coarse	bumpy, rough	fine, smooth
colossal	enormous, immense	tiny, insignificant, trivial
combine	blend, unite, join	separate
comical	amusing, funny	tragic, sorrowful
complex	complicated, intricate	simple
competent	capable, qualified	incompetent, inept
comprehend	understand, grasp	confuse, misinterpret
complete	conclude, finish	incomplete
complex	complicated, intricate	simple
compress	crush, condense	expand
concrete	real, tangible, solid	abstract, flimsy
concur	agree, cooperate	disagree
condemn	censure, denounce	approve
condense	compress, concentrate	expand, enlarge
confess	admit, acknowledge	deny
confine	contain, enclose, restrain	free, release
conflict	oppose, differ, clash	agree
conflict	fight, battle, struggle	peace, harmony
conform	comply, submit	dissent, dispute
confuse	complicate, muddle	clarify
congested	overcrowded, stuffed	empty, unfilled
connect	join, link, attach	separate, disconnect

conscientious	scrupulous, virtuous	neglectful, careless
conscious	aware, cognizant	unaware, unconscious
consecutive	successive, continuous	interrupted
conservative	cautious, restrained	radical, extreme
considerate	thoughtful, sympathetic	thoughtless, selfish
constantly	always, continually	scarcely, seldom
contaminate	pollute, defile, infect	purify
contented	satisfied, pleased	dissatisfied, unhappy
continue	persist, persevere	discontinue, stop
convalesce	recuperate, recover, heal	relapse
convenient	handy, accessible	inconvenient
conventional	customary, traditional	unusual
correct	accurate, right, proper	wrong, incorrect
courage	bravery, valour	cowardice
courteous	polite, civil	rude
dally	loiter, linger	rush
damage	hurt, impair, harm	remedy, repair
dangerous	unsafe, hazardous	safe
daring	bold, audacious	cautious
dark	dismal, black	light
dawn	daybreak, sunrise	evening
dead	lifeless, deceased	alive, active
decay	rot, spoil	bloom, flourish
deduct	subtract, remove	add
defend	protect, shield	attack, assault
defy	resist, challenge	obeys, comply
delicate	fragile, dainty	sturdy
demolish	destroy, wreck	restore
denounce	blame, censure, indict	commend
dense	thick, compressed	sparse, empty
depart	leave, exit	arrive
deposit	store, place	withdraw
desolate	barren, forsaken	dense, verdant
early	premature, beforetime	late
easy	Simple	hard
eccentric	peculiar, unusual	normal
ecstasy	joy, rapture, elation	sadness, depression
empty	drain, unload	fill

encourage	promote, support, urge	discourage
enemy	opponent, foe	ally, friend
enjoy	like, appreciate	dislike, hate
enlarge	expand, magnify	reduce, shrink
enormous	vast, immense, colossal	tiny, microscopic
enough	sufficient, ample, plenty	insufficient
entirely	wholly, completely	partly
eternal	always, perpetual	temporary, passing
evident	apparent, obvious, clear	doubtful, vague
evil	bad, wrong, wicked	good
exceptional	remarkable, outstanding	ordinary, commonplace
excite	arouse, provoke, incite	compose, calm
exhilarated	overjoyed, ecstatic	depressed, dejected, sad
explicit	exact, distinct	indefinite, unclear
exquisite	delightful, charming	revolting, repulsive
exterior	outside, outer	interior
extravagant	extreme, excessive,	meagre
fabulous	marvellous, amazing	unexciting
face	confront, meet	avoid
fair	honest, just, impartial	unjust, unfair
fake	imitation, phoney	real, genuine
false	incorrect, untrue	true
fancy	elaborate, ornate, fussy	simple, plain
fantastic	incredible, outrageous	ordinary, usual
fast	rapid, quick, swift	slow
fat	chubby, plump, stout	thin
fatal	deadly, mortal, killing	harmless
fatigue	tiredness, exhaust	energy, freshness
feasible	possible, attainable	impossible
feeble	weak, frail	strong
ferocious	fierce, savage, brutal	tame, gentle
fertile	fruitful, productive	unproductive, barren
fiction	fantasy, untruth, myth	truth
fill	load, pack	empty
fix	mend, repair	break
flaw	defect, fault, blemish	perfection
flimsy	frail, fragile, delicate	sturdy, strong
flippant	impudent, sassy	polite, respectful

fluid	Liquid	solid
foe	enemy, adversary	friend
gain	acquire, obtain, receive	lose
gallant	chivalrous, stately	ungentlemanly
gather	collect, accumulate	scatter, disperse
gaudy	showy, garish, vulgar	tasteful, refined
gaunt	scrawny, skinny, thin	overweight, plump
generous	giving, selfless	selfish, stingy
gentle	tender, mild	rough, harsh
genuine	real, authentic, sincere	fake, phoney
gigantic	immense, colossal	tiny, minute
give	donate, present, offer	take, receive
glad	happy, pleased	sad, unhappy
gloomy	dark, dismal, depressing	cheery, bright
glorious	splendid, magnificent	terrible, awful
good	nice, fine, well-behaved	bad, awful
gorgeous	ravishing, dazzling	hideous, unattractive
gratitude	thankfulness, appreciation	ungratefulness
great	outstanding, remarkable	insignificant, unimportant
hate	loathe, detest	love
help	aid, assist	hinder, thwart
high	elevated, lofty	low
hold	grasp, grip, retain	release, discharge
honest	truthful, sincere, frank	untruthful, insincere
hospitable	welcoming, cordial	rude, unfriendly
hostile	antagonistic, aggressive	friendly, cordial
huge	vast, immense, great	small, tiny
humble	modest, unpretentious	vain, showy
humiliate	embarrass, disgrace	honour, dignify
identical	alike, duplicate	different, varied
idle	inactive, lazy	busy, ambitious
ignorant	uninformed, unaware	knowledgeable
immaculate	spotless, pure	dirty, filthy
immature	childish, inexperienced	mature, adult
immune	resistant, exempt	susceptible
impartial	neutral, unbiased, fair	prejudiced
impatient	eager, anxious	patient
imperative	compulsory, crucial	unnecessary, optional

imperfect	marred, defective, faulty	perfect, flawless
impetuous	impulsive, rash, reckless	restrained, careful
important	significant, meaningful	unimportant, meaningless
independent	self-reliant, autonomous	dependent, unsure
inferior	lesser, substandard	superior
infuriate	enrage, agitate, provoke	soothe, clam
ingenious	clever, creative, original	unoriginal, dull
intelligent	bright, sensible, rational	ignorant, dense
interesting	provocative, engrossing	dull, boring
intermittent	sporadic, periodic	regular, continual
internal	inner, inside	external, outer
intolerant	bigoted, prejudiced	understanding, accepting
intriguing	fascinating, enthralling	uninteresting, dull
join	connect, unite, link	separate, disconnect
jolly	merry, jovial, joyful	sad, grim, glum
jubilant	overjoyed, delighted	dejected, depressed
keep	save, protect, guard	discard, lose
kind	considerate, tender	mean, inconsiderate
lament	mourn, grieve	rejoice, celebrate
large	big. massive, huge	small, little
last	final, end	first, beginning
least	fewest, minimum	most, maximum
legible	readable, clear	illegible, unreadable
lenient	lax, unrestrained, easy	harsh, strict
listless	lethargic, tired	active, energetic
logical	sensible, sane, rational	illogical, unreasonable
long	Lengthy	short
loose	slack, limp	tight
lure	attract, seduce, entice	repel
luxurious	extravagant, elegant	meagre, scanty
magnify	expand, enlarge	reduce, minimize
mandatory	required, compulsory	optional
manoeuvre	manipulate, handle,	scheme
maximum	greatest, uppermost	minimum, least
meagre	scanty, sparse, poor	abundant, generous
mean	unkind, malicious, nasty	pleasant, nice
mediocre	fair, moderate, so-so	outstanding
mend	repair, fix	break

migrant	drifting, travelling	stationary, immovable
militant	combative, aggressive	peaceful
minor	lesser, inferior	major
mirth	merriment, fun, laughter	gloom, sadness
mischievous	naughty, impish	well-behaved, angelic
misfortune	hardship, catastrophe	good luck, fortune
naughty	bad, disobedient, wrong	good, appropriate
neat	clean, orderly, tidy	sloppy, disorderly
negligent	careless, derelict	conscientious, careful
nervous	ruffled, flustered	composed, calm
neutral	impartial, unprejudiced	prejudiced, partial
new	unused, fresh, modern	old, antique
nice	pleasing, desirable, fine	unpleasant, naughty
nonchalant	indifferent, blasé	concerned, apprehensive
normal	ordinary, typical, usual	abnormal, unusual
numerous	several, abundant	few, scanty
obey	mind, heed, comply	disobey, resist
oblivious	unconscious, dazed	mindful, aware
obnoxious	offensive, abominable	pleasant, pleasing
observe	examine, study	ignore, disregard
obsolete	extinct, antiquated	stylish, vogue, current
opponent	enemy, rival, foe	ally, friend
optimistic	hopeful, confident	pessimistic
optional	voluntary, elective	required
ordinary	usual, average	unusual, remarkable
outrageous	preposterous, shocking	warranted, acceptable
outstanding	extraordinary, distinguished	insignificant, inconsequential
painstaking	meticulous, precise	careless, negligent
passive	compliant, submissive	forceful
past	former, previous	future
patience	tolerance, perseverance	impatience
peculiar	weird, bizarre	normal, conventional
perfect	flawless, accurate	imperfect, faulty
permanent	enduring, lasting	temporary, changing
perpetual	eternal, endless	short-lived, fleeting
persuade	convince, influence	dissuade, deter
plausible	believable, reasonable	unbelievable

plentiful	ample, enough	scarce, insufficient
pliable	supple, flexible	rigid, closed-minded
polite	gracious, refined	rude, discourteous
poor	destitute, needy	rich, wealthy
portion	part, segment, piece	whole, total
possible	conceivable, feasible	impossible, unachievable
precarious	dangerous, uncertain	sure, safe
precious	cherished, valuable	cheap, worthless
prejudiced	biased, opinionated	impartial
premature	early, hasty	late, delayed
premeditated	planned, intended	spontaneous, accidental
preserve	uphold, guard, save	destroy, neglect
pretty	lovely, beautiful	homely, unattractive
prevalent	customary, widespread	uncommon, unusual
prevent	thwart, prohibit, hinder	permit, allow
qualified	competent, suited	unfit, unsuited
question	interrogates, inquire	answer
quiet	silent, hushed, tranquil	noisy, rowdy
quit	cease, stop, withdraw	continue, remain
radiant	luminous, shining	dim, not illuminated
raise	hoist, elevate	lower
ratify	approve, confirm	veto, refuse
rational	logical, level-headed	irrational, crazy
ravage	devastates, ruin, damage	restore, revitalize
raze	destroy, demolish	build, construct
recreation	amusement, pleasure	work, labour
reduce	lessen, decrease	increase, enlarge
refute	contradict, dispute	agree, concur
regular	routine, customary	irregular, abnormal
regulate	control, oversee	decontrol
relentless	persistent, merciless	lenient, sympathetic
relevant	pertinent, suitable	irrelevant, insignificant
reliable	trustworthy, steadfast	undependable, unreliable
reluctant	unwilling, hesitant	willing, accommodating
remote	secluded, isolated	close, accessible
repulsive	hideous, offensive	pleasing, alluring
reputable	honourable, upstanding	dishonest, untrustworthy
resist	oppose, withstand, defy	comply, conform

reveal	show, disclose, divulge	hide, conceal
ridiculous	nonsensical, foolish	sensible, believable
risky	hazardous, perilous	safe, sound
same	identical, alike	different, diverse
savage	uncivilized, barbarous	civilized, gentle, tame
save	preserve, conserve, keep	spend, discard
scarce	scanty, rare, sparse	plentiful, abundant
scrawny	skinny, gaunt, spindly	husky, chubby
scrupulous	meticulous, ethical	unethical, careless
seize	apprehend, grab, snatch	release, free
separate	divide, segregate	unite, join
serene	peaceful, tranquil, calm	disturbed, upset
serious	grave, solemn, pensive	flighty, fickle
shrewd	clever, cunning, crafty	unthinking, careless
special	exceptional, notable	ordinary, usual
spontaneous	instinctive, automatic	planned, rehearsed
stable	steady, unchanging	unsettled
stationary	fixed, immobile, firm	movable, portable
stimulate	rouse, stir, motivate	stifle, suppress
stop	quit, cease, terminate	start, begin
strenuous	vigorous, laborious	effortless, easy
strict	stringent, severe, stern	lenient
strong	powerful, mighty, potent	weak
stupid	unintelligent, dense	knowledgeable, smart
subsequent	following, succeeding	preceding, previous
successful	thriving, prosperous	failing, unsuccessful
sufficient	ample, enough, adequate	lacking, insufficient
superb	magnificent, exquisite	inferior, mediocre
suppress	restrain, inhibit, squelch	foster, encourage
tall	high, lofty	short
tangible	concrete, definite	vague, ambiguous
taut	tense, tight, stiff	relaxed
tender	delicate, gentle	harsh, rough
terrible	dreadful, horrible	wonderful, superb
thaw	melt, defrost	freeze
thrifty	economical, frugal	wasteful, extravagant
thrive	prosper, flourish	fail, fade, shrivel
total	whole, entire, complete	partial

trivial	insignificant, worthless	important, crucial
turbulent	tumultuous, blustering	clam, peaceful
turmoil	commotion, disturbance	quiet, tranquillity
unbiased	impartial, unprejudiced	prejudiced, partial
upset	perturb, ruffle, agitate	soothe, calm
urgent	crucial, important	unimportant, trivial
vacant	unoccupied, empty	filled, occupied
vague	unclear, obscure	clear, definite
valiant	courageous, brave	cowardly, fearful
vibrate	shake, quiver, tremble	firm, steady
vicious	malicious, spiteful	kind, humane
victory	triumph, win, success	defeat
virtuous	moral, righteous, angelic	sinful, wicked
vulgar	offensive, uncouth	refined, tasteful
wealth	riches, prosperity, assets	poverty
weary	tired, fatigued, lethargic	energetic, lively
wholehearted	earnest, sincere	insincere
wild	uncivilized, savage	tame, calm
win	triumph, succeed	lose
wise	knowing, scholarly	dull, uneducated
wonderful	marvellous, incredible	ordinary, blah
worn	used, impaired, old	new, fresh
wrong	incorrect, untrue	correct, right
yield	produce, bear, provide	keep, retain
yoke	bond, connect, hitch	unhitch
youth	adolescent, youngster	adulthood
zany	amusing, funny, comical	serious
zest	charm, appetite	apathy
zealous	ardent, fervent, militant	apathetic, indifferent
zenith	peak, pinnacle, summit	bottom, base

5

One Word Substitution

One word may be used in place of several words or phrases. This will help us in being concise. Table 5.1 contains a lengthy list of one word substitutions.

Table 5.1: List of One Word Substitution

Phrase	One Word
A border separating two countries	Frontier
A country ruled by two country	Condominium
A collection of poems or other pieces of writing	Anthology
A dramatic performance	Masque
A very deep hole	Abyss
A lady's purse	Reticule
A group of people who sing together	Chorus
A man of odd habits	Eccentric
A man who dances to the tunes of his wife	Henpecked
A minor illness	Ailment
A mistaken idea or belief	Fallacy
A nation engaged in war	Belligerent
A new word or expression	Neologism
A period of 1,000 years	Millennium
A person behind time	Antiquated
A person who can travel in space	Astronaut
A person who wishes to throw his establishment	Anarchist
A person who helps another commit crime	Accomplice
A person gives money or other help	Benefactor
A person who lives at the same time	Contemporary
A person who kills a king	Regicide
A place of good climate	Sanatorium
A place of washing dishes adjoining kitchen	Scullery
A place where public records are kept and preserved	Archives

A religious song	Hymn
A remarkable talent	Prodigy
A remedy for all diseases	Panacea
A short but amusing story	Anecdote
A speech or piece of writing expressing praise	Encomium
A standard by which something may be judged	Criterion
A state of long-lasting unconsciousness	Coma
A verse letter	Epistle
A war between the people of the same country	Civil war
A writer who uses others ideas and words as if they were his own	Plagiarist
Act of killing one's wife	Uxoricide
An animal story with a moral	Fable
An animal living on another	Parasite
An extremely stupid behaviour	Idiocy
An extreme poverty	Penury
An instrument for viewing objects at a distance	Telescope
An open rebellion against authority	Mutiny
An unknown person	Anonymous
Animals living on land and in water	Amphibian
Appointment by two parties to settle a dispute	Arbiter
Art of cutting tree and bushes into ornamental shape	Topiary
At the same time	Contemporary
Award given after death	Posthumous
Based on experience or observation rather than theory	Empirical
Borrow ideas and steal others words is called	Plagiarism
Calm and peaceful	Serene
Care taker of a public building	Custodian
Change one's mind too quickly	Vacillation
Cheerful and friendly	Jovial
Complete disorder and confusion	Chaos
Congratulate somebody in formal manner	Felicitate
Concise and exact use of words	Brevity
Contempt of God	Blasphemy
Creature having both male and female organs	Hermaphrodite
A citizen of the world	Cosmopolite
Cure for all disease	Panacea

Custom of having many husbands	Polyandry
Custom of having many wives	Polygamy
Dealing of counterfeit things	Forgery
Disease which is spread by contact	Contagious
Doctor who treats children	Paediatrician
Earliest inhabitants of a region	Aborigines
Easy to understand or clear	Lucid
Equal in rank	Peer
Eating great quantities of food	Voracious
Express in a strong disagreement or disapproval	Expostulate
Express strong protest	Fulminate
Extremely impressive and attractive	Stunning
Extremely unwilling to spend money	Parsimony
Extremely desirous for money	Avarious
Excessive false praise	Flattery
Fault that may be forgiven	Venial
Favouring own kith and kin	Nepotism
Fear of bathing	Ablutophobia
Fear of becoming bald	Phalacrophobia
Fear of being robbed	Harpaxophobia
Fear of cockroaches	Katsaridaphobia
Fear of crowd	Ochlophobia
Fear of darkness	Lygophobia
Fear of death	Nicrophobia
Fear of dentist	Dentophobia
Fear of disease	Pathophobia
Fear of failure	Atychiphobia
Fear of foreigners	Xenophobia
Fear of God	Zeusophobia
Fear of going to bed	Clinophobia
Fear of height	Acrophobia
Fear of making decisions	Decidophobia
Fear of poverty	Peniaphobia
Fear of property	Orthophobia
Fear of radiation	Radiophobia
Fear of riding a car	Amaxophobia
Fear of school	Scolionophobia
Fear of sex	Genophobia

Fear of speaking	Lalophobia
Fear of speed	Tachophobia
Fear of water	Hydrophobia
Fear of words	Logophobia
First speech	Maiden
Food agrees with one's taste	Palatable
Forbidden by law, rules	Illicit
Funny imitation of a poem	Parody
Giving a lot of information in a few words clearly	Concise
Giving up throne by the king	Abdication
Go back and forth	Shuttle
Government by a single person	Autocracy
Government by the Gods	Theocracy
Government runs by a dictator	Autocracy
Great enthusiasm and energy	Zest
Group of three novels	Trilogy
Having too much interest in sexual matters	Salacious
Hard to understand	Obscure
Impossible to understand or interpret	Inscrutable
Incapable of being wounded	Invulnerable
In-charge of museum /Pitch	Curator
Indifference to pleasure or pain	Stoicism
Instruments which makes smaller objects larger	Microscope
Intentional destruction of racial group	Genocide
Intended to be kept secret	Confidential
Interval between two events	Interlude
Just punishment for wrong doing	Nemesis
Keeping careful watch	Vigilant
Killing of another human being	Homicide
Knowing and using several languages	Polyglot
Lack of belief in God	Atheist
Language difficult to understand	Jargon
Large scale departure of people	Exodus
Leaving a meet as an expression of disapproval	Walkout
List of explanation of words	Glossary
List of goods with their price	Invoice
Longing for something	Nostalgia
Loop of rope is called	Noose

Loud talk or speech	Harangue
Made or done by someone whose name is not known	Anonymous
Man having the qualities of woman	Effeminate
Man of lax moral	Licentious
Man whose wife has been unfaithful to him	Cuckold
Mania for setting fires	Pyromania
Mania for stealing things	Kleptomania
Mania for talking	Logo mania
Mania for travel	Dromomania
Mania of being important	Megalomania
Medicine which lessens pain	Anodyne
Member of a band of robbers	Brigand
Morning Prayer	Matin
Moving towards a centre	Centripetal
Murdering of a family	Familicide
Murdering of an infant	Infanticide
Murdering of Brother	Fratricide
Murdering of husband by his wife	Mariticide
Murdering of the king	Regicide
Murdering of tyrant	Tyrannicide
Not able to be recovered or changed	Irrevocable
Occurring at the end of a process or period of time	Eventual
Officially declare free from blame	Exonerate
Officially reject a legal decision	Quash
Of the sky or heaven	Celestial
Of major importance or historic	Epoch-making
Old age when a man behaves like a fool	Dotage
One who believes one is	God Theo mania
One who believes that everything is pre-destined	Fatalist
One who believes that pleasure is the chief good	Hedonist
One who believes in fate	Fatalist
One who betrays one	Traitor
One who collects coins	Numismatist
One who comes from a village and considered stupid	Bumpkin
One who compiles dictionary	Lexicographer
One who cuts precious stones	Lapidist

One who deserts his religion	Apostate
One who does not care for literature	Philistine
One who does not respect something sacred or holy	Blasphemy
One who does not take a definite stand	Evasive
One who draws maps and charts	Cartographer
One who eats everything	Omnivorous
One who eats human flesh	Cannibal
One who fights for the sake of money	Mercenary
One who forsakes religion	Renegade
One who has many talents	Versatile
One who has suddenly gained new wealth	Parvenu
One who has unreasoning enthusiasm for the glorification of one's country	Chauvinism
One who hates knowledge and learning	Misologist
One who is bad in spelling	Cacographic
One who is guilty of firing property	Arsonist
One who is more interested in himself	Introvert
One who is more interested in others	Extrovert
One who is neither intelligent nor dull	Mediocre
One who is not the citizen of country	Alien
One who is talkative	Garrulous
One who is the most powerful	Omnipotent
One who is very careful and particular	Meticulous
One who is very well versed in any subject	Connoisseur
One who lends money at high rate	Usurer
One who loves all and sundry	Philanthropist
One who loves books	Bibliophile
One who passes through the gate without taking permission	Trespasser
One who pays too much attention to his clothes and appearance	Dandy
One who plays a game for pleasure not professionally	Amateur
One who pretends illness to escape duty	Malingerer
One who reads only books	Bookworm
One who sacrifices his life for country	Martyr
One who sneaks into a country	Infiltrator
One who speaks many languages	Polyglot

One who studies skin and its diseases	Dermatologist
One who studies the formation of the earth	Geologist
One who talks continuously	Loquacious
One who thinks human nature is evil	Cynic
One who totally abstain from alcohol	Teetotaller
One who travels from place to place	Itinerant
One who treats female problems	Gynaecologist
One who wants to see others unhappy	Sadist
One who works in return for being taught the trade	Disciple
One who works without getting any salary	Honorary
One whose attitude is to eat, drink and merry	Epicurean
Opposing arguments	Rebut
Out of date things	Obsolescent
Paper written in one's own handwriting	Manuscript
Part of a church in which bells are hung	Belfry
Partly male and partly female	Androgynous
People in rowdy scene	Rabble
Person different to pleasure and pain	Stoic
Person obsessed with one idea or subject	Monomaniac
Person pretending to be somebody he is not	Impostor
Person who believes God is everything	Ban theist
Person who believes others	Credulous
Person who does not believe in any religion	Pagan
Person who enjoys sensuous enjoyments	Epicure
Person who has long experience	Veteran
Person who hates women	Misogynist
Person who holds scholarship at a university	Bursar
Person who is against ordinary society especially dressing	Hippy
Person who is always dissatisfied	Malcontent
Person who is made to bear the blame	Scapegoat
Person who kill others for political reason	Assassin
Person who lives alone and avoids other people	Recluse
Person who loves nature	Aesthete
Person who makes love for amusement	Philanderer
Person who pretends to have more knowledge	Charlatan
Person who regards the whole world as his country	Cosmopolitan
Person with a beautiful handwriting	Calligrapher

Person without manners	Rustic
Persuasive and fluent speech	Eloquence
Physician who delivers babies	Obstetrician
Place where birds are kept	Aviary
Place where cows are sheltered	Byre
Place where government records are kept	Archives
Place where women dwelled (Ancient time)	Harem
Place which provides both board and lodging	Inn
Plants and vegetation	Flora
Poem narrating a popular story	Ballad
Poem written on the death of someone loved and lost	Elegy
Policy of political party	Manifesto
Power of reading thoughts of others	Telepathy
Present and explain systematically	Expound
Printed notice in a newspaper of somebody's death and details of his life	Obituary
Public building where weapons are made and stored	Arsenal
Quick and efficient	Expeditious
Regard with great respect	Venerate
Relating to more than one department	Interdisciplinary
Relax completely	Veg
Responsible according to law	Legitimate
Ride on someone else back	Piggyback
Ridiculous use of words	Malapropism
Room leading into a large room	Anteroom
Room with toilet facilities	Lavatory
Rude and lacking consideration of others	Discourteous
School for infants and children	Kindergarten
Seat on elephant's back	Howdah
Send unwanted person out of the country	Deport
Sexually immoral	Licentious
Short journey made by a group of persons together	Excursion
Short remaining end of cigarette	Stub
Short walk for pleasure or exercise	Stroll
Slow witted person	Duffer
Showing dedication or great care	Sedulous

Song sung at burial	Dirge
Speech by an actor at the end of a play	Epilogue
Speech without preparation	Extempore
Stage between boyhood and youth	Adolescence
Statement which cannot be understood	Incomprehensible
Stories of old time Gods and heroes	Legend
Story that cannot be believed	Incredible
Strongly urge to do something	Exhort
Study of ancient science	Archaeology
Study of birds	Ornithologist
Study of human body	Anatomy
Study of mankind	Anthropology
Study of statistics of birth, death and diseases	Demography
Sudden rush of winds	Gust
That impossible or hard to believe	Incredible
That impossible to travel along or over	Impassable
That cannot be avoided	Inevitable
That which is incapable of making mistakes	Infallible
That which cannot be imitated	Inimitable
The scientific study of weather	Meteorology
The ability to speak clever amusing things	Wit
The belief that God exists	Theism
The study of God and religious belief	Theology
The study of signs and symbols	Semiotics
The study of speech sounds	Phonetics
The concluding part of a speech	Peroration
The belief that God is present in all things	Pantheism
The belief that nothing has any value	Nihilism
The origin of something	Genesis
The ending of a law, system, or custom	Abolition
The theory of law	Jurisprudence
Think deeply about something	Ruminate
Thing that bring gentle and painless death from incurable death	Euthanasia
Thing that cannot be touched of felt	Palpable
Thing that destroys the effect of poison	Antidote
Thing through which light cannot pass	Opaque
Thing which cannot be done without	Indispensable

Things that can be seen and touched	Tangible
Things that cannot be understood	Unintelligible
To come into a country	Immigrant
To do away with a rule	Abrogate
To explain a spiritual truth	Parable
To spread troops for battle	Deploy
Too great for words	Ineffable
Tumour which is not likely to spread	Benign
Unable to be trusted	Treacherous
Unexpected stroke of good luck	Windfall
Using of new words	Neology
Unwilling to speak frankly	Mealy-mouthed
Very rich, elaborate, or luxurious	Lavish
Very fond of drinking alcohol	Bibulous
Views which are not of one's liking	Irritating
Walking in sleep	Somnambulism
Which cannot be rectified	Irreparable
Without moral principle	Unscrupulous
Woman who has extra marital relationship	Adultery
Work which involves too much official formalities	Red-tapism

6

Homophones

When writing a paper, it is very important to choose the correct words so that the reader can understand what you, the writer, want to tell them. There is one category of words that can be difficult to use correctly: homophones.

Homophones are a group of words that sound the same when they are said aloud, but have different spellings and meanings. They can also be different parts of speech. When using a word that is a homophone, it is important to know the meaning of each word, so that you can choose the one you want.

A detailed list of homophones with their meaning is given below.

Amend: to improve something.
Emend: to remove errors from a text.

Artist: someone who paints or makes sculptures.
Artiste: a skilled performer, especially a dancer.

Aloud: speaking audibly.
Allowed: permitted.

Ascent: the action of going up.
Assent: approval.

Autarchy: despotism.
Autarky: economic self-sufficiency.

Board: a flat piece of wood.
Bored: not interested in something.

Beech: a kind of tree.
Beach: sea shore.

Birth: born.
Berth: with bed.

Bare: empty/plain.

Bear: carry/endure.

Bail: on condition let out.
Bale: bundle.

Ball: football.
Bawl: shouted.

Brake: stop.
Break: make into pieces.

Bolder: more courageous.
Boulder: a large smooth rock.

Boarder: a pupil who lives in a boarding school.
Border: line dividing two countries.

Born: come to life.
Borne: carried.

Beat: to strike.
Beet: a vegetable.

Be: to exit.
Bee: an insect.

By: at.
Bye: by the way.
Buy: to purchase.

Canon: principle.
Cannon: gun.

Cast: throw.
Caste: sect or community.

Compliment: praise.
Complement: which completes.

Confirm: ratify.
Conform: comply with.

Council: assembly.
Counsel: advice.

Carrier: one who carries goods.
Career: mode of living.

Canvas: rough cloth.
Canvass: asking for vote.

Ceiling: to cover upper surface.
Sealing: stamp.

Cereal: food grain rich in carbohydrate.
Serial: forming a series.

Check: examine or control.
Cheque: bank written order.

Cell: small room.
Sell: exchange things for money.

Cue: signal.
Queue: a line of people.

Course: a series of lessons.
Coarse: having a rough texture.

Chord: a group of notes sounded together.
Cord: a string.

Desert: dry area of land covered with sand.
Dessert: the last part of a meal.

Dual: double.
Duel: fight.

Disease: sickness.
Decease: death.

Die: death.
Dye: colour.

Dear: much loved.
Deer: a hoofed animal.

Dose: a quantity of medicine usually taken at a time.
Doze: sleep lightly.

Draught: a movement of air.
Drought: a period of time when there is little or no rain.

Fourth: one of four equal parts.
Forth: forward.

Fair: good.
Fare: charge.

Grate: make harsh sound.
Great: famous.

Hear: to be aware of sound.
Here: a specific location.

Hole: an opening.
Whole: all of something.

In: preposition used to describe the position of a thing.
Inn: hotel.

Know: to have information or knowledge in your mind.
No: used to give a negative answer or reply.

Knight: soldier of a cavalry.
Night: darkness.

Lessen: to diminish.
Lesson: task.

Latter: towards the end.
Later: next.

Loath: unwilling.
Loathe: disliking greatly.

Meter: measurer.
Metre: measure in poetry.

Meat: the flesh of animals or birds used as food.
Meet: come to face to face.

Minor: little in importance.
Miner: a person who works in a mine.

Not: no.
Knot: tied together.

Pear: to cut or trim.
Pair: a set of two of same thing which are used together.

Peace: freedom from war.
Piece: a part of anything.

Pray: to speak reverently to God.
Prey: a bird or animal.

Review: a survey or report.
Revue: a musical show.

Roll: list of names.
Role: a part played by an actor.

Right: correct.
Write: to form numbers or words using a pen, pencil etc.

Steal: to take without permission.
Steel: a very hard alloy of iron and carbon.

Stationery: writing material.
Stationary: fixed.

Seen: third form of the verb 'see'.
Scene: the place where something real/imaginary happens.

Sight: act of seeing.
Cite: mention as an example.
Site: chosen ground.

Sent: cause to go.
Scent: perfume.

Soul: the spirit.
Sole: only/single.

Stair: a number of steps.
Stare: to look at something.

Their: relating or belonging to certain people, animals, or things.
There: a specific place or location.

To: used to indicate the place, person, or thing that something moves toward.
Too: more than what is wanted, accepted, needed, possible etc.

Troop: company of persons or animals.
Troup: company of actors.

Week: unit of time.
Weak: becoming pale.

Whether: a conjunction used to talk about a choice or doubt
Weather: a noun used to talk about rain, snow, sun etc.

Wait: defer action for a specified time.
Weight: force experienced by a body as a result of Earth's gravitation.

7

Rules of Sentence Structure

A sentence is a group of words that makes a complete sense. Generally, we know that a sentence consists of two parts. These two parts of a sentence are the *subject part* and the *predicate part*.

The subject is usually a noun—a word that names a person, place, or thing—or a noun phrase. Generally, the subject of a sentence tells who or what the sentence is about. The subject is the noun or noun phrase that is doing something in the sentence.

The predicate is—besides the 'subject' the remaining words that express an action, existence (a state of being), or an occurrence—or a verb phrase. The predicate usually follows the subject and tells what the subject does or what it is like.

7.1 Kinds of Sentences

Sentences are of three kinds according to their structure:

1. Simple sentence (contains one clause).
2. Compound sentence (more than one clause).
3. Complex sentence (more than one clause).

Clause: A clause is a simple sentence with a subject and a verb in the predicate part. There are two kinds of clauses: independent and dependent.

An *independent clause* contains a subject and a verb and expresses a complete thought. It can stand alone as a sentence by itself. An independent clause is formed with a subject and a verb and often a complement.

A *dependent clause* begins with a subordinator such as when, while, if, that, or who. A dependent clause does not express a complete thought, so it is not a sentence by itself. A dependent clause is also called a sentence fragment. By itself, it is an incomplete sentence, and it is an error. A dependent clause is formed with a subordinator, a subject, and a verb.

Subordinators: After, before, that, when, which, although, even though, though, whenever, while as, just as, how, unless, where, who, as if, if, until, wherever, whom, as soon as, since, what, whether, whose, because, so that.

7.1.1 Simple Sentences: Simple sentences have one subject/verb pair. Verbs must agree with their subjects in number and person.

- Marie runs.
- We run.

Even though the subject may be more than one person or thing, and the predicate may contain more than one verb or action, a sentence will still be a simple sentence if it only has one subject/verb pair.

- Marie and I run and win.

Simple sentences may also contain an object. The object is part of the predicate. It is usually a noun that follows the verb and receives the action of the verb.

- Marie runs the race.

Simple sentences may also contain modifiers that describe the subject or predicate.

- My sister Marie runs the race quickly.

A subject/predicate pair that can stand on its own is an independent clause. A simple sentence consists of just one independent clause.

A. Kinds of Simple Sentences: Simple sentences may be of the following kinds:

- Declarative sentence.
- Interrogative sentence.
- Imperative sentence.
- Exclamatory sentence.

A declarative sentence states a fact in the affirmative or negative form.

For example:

- This is a museum (+)

- She is not a student (–)

Negative sentences are formed by means of the negative particle *not* which is put after the verb (auxiliary, modal, link verb).

- For example: I do not like rainy weather.

Negative pronouns (no-one, none, neither, nothing, no, etc.), negative adverbs (never, nowhere, etc.) and some other words (hardly, refuse, without, etc.) are also used to express negation.

There is only one negation in an English sentence.

Interrogative sentences ask questions and have the following two forms:

Yes/No Questions: Questions asked by different auxiliaries.

Wh-questions: Questions asked by wh-words.

For example:

- Do you like sweets?
- Is he a singer?
- What is your name?
- How old are you?

Imperative sentences express commands, requests, invitations, etc.

For example:

- Stand up.
- Open the door.

An exclamatory sentence expresses some kind of emotion or feeling (joy, anger, grief, wonder, etc.). It often begins with the words *what* and *how*.

For example:

- How wonderful!
- What fine weather we are having today!

7.1.2 Compound Sentences: A compound sentence has two independent clauses. An independent clause is a part of a sentence that can stand alone because it contains a subject and a verb and expresses a complete thought. Basically, a compound contains two simple sentences. These independent clauses are joined by a conjunction (for, and, nor, but, or, yet, so). These are called co-coordinating conjunctions.

- They spoke to him in Spanish, but he responded in English.
- He worked hard and got a scholarship.

There are three ways to join the clauses: With a coordinator:

- Salt water boils at a higher temperature than freshwater, so food cooks faster in salt water.

Construction:

Independent clause + coordinator + independent clause

There are seven coordinators, which are also called coordinating conjunctions. You can remember them by the phrase FANBOYS (For, And, Nor, But, Or, Yet, So).

- For: to add a reason
- And: to add a similar, equal idea
- Nor: to add a negative equal idea
- But: to add an opposite idea
- Or: to add an alternative possibility
- Yet: to add an unexpected or surprising continuation
- So: to add an expected result

With a conjunctive adverb:

- Salt water boils at a higher temperature than fresh water; *therefore,* food cooks faster in salt water.

Construction:

Independent clause + conjunctive adverb + independent clause

Several transition signals, such as *on the other hand, as a result*, and *for example*, act like conjunctive adverbs; they can also connect independent clauses with a semi-colon and a comma.

Also, besides, furthermore, in addition, moreover, as well, too, add a similar, equal idea.

However, nevertheless, nonetheless, still, add an unexpected or surprising continuation.

On the other hand, in contrast–to add a complete contrast.

Otherwise–to give an alternative possibility.

For example, for instance–to add an example.

As a result, consequently, hence, therefore, thus, add to an expected result.

With a Semicolon: Salt water boils at a higher temperature than fresh water; food cooks faster in salt water.

This kind of compound sentence is possible only when the two independent clauses are closely related in meaning. If they are not closely related, they should be written as two simple sentences, each ending with a period.

7.1.3 Complex Sentences: A complex sentence is an independent clause joined by one or more dependent clauses. A dependent clause either lacks a subject or a verb or has both a subject and a verb that does not express a complete thought. A complex sentence always has a subordinator (as, because, since, after, although, when) or relative pronouns (who, that, which).

After eating lunch at The Cheesecake Factory, Tim went to the gym to exercise.

A. Complex Sentences with Adverb Clauses: An adverb clause acts like an adverb; that is, it tells where, when, why, and how. An adverb clause begins with a subordinator, such as *when, while, because, although, if, so,* or *that*. It can come before or after an independent clause.

B. Complex Sentences with Adjective Clauses: An adjective clause acts like an adjective; that is, it describes a noun or a pronoun. An adjective clause begins with a relative pronoun, such as *who, whom, which, whose,* or *that*, or with a relative adverb, such as *where or when*. It follows the noun or pronoun it describes.

C. Complex Sentences with Noun Clauses: A noun clause begins with a *wh-* question word, *that, whether*, and sometimes *if.* A noun clause acts like a noun; it can be either the subject or an object of the independent clause.

D. Compound-Complex Sentences: A compound-complex sentence has two independent clauses and at least one dependent clause. One can use almost any combination of dependent and independent clauses.

The man believed in the system, and he knew that justice would prevail after the murderer was sent to jail.

7.2 Syntax

The word *syntax* is derived from the Greek word *suntaxis*. It is a technical term for the rules governing the way words in any language are put together into sentences. Syntax is particularly important in English, where a small change in word order can completely change the meaning of the sentence. For example, 'The doctor saw the patient' is different from 'The patient saw the doctor'—same words, different order, and very different meaning (Incidentally, this is another example of an incomplete sentence)! Syntax is about paying attention to word order (and therefore sentence meaning). This can be particularly difficult for people who use English as a second language, partly because most speakers of any language usually learn basic syntax as they grow up surrounded by the language, and partly because other languages have other ways of indicating the meaning.

Word order in ancient Greek, for example, was largely irrelevant, and other aspects of grammar made the meaning perfectly clear. This is not the case in English. Word order is absolutely crucial for clarity, accuracy and meaning. The rules of syntax are notoriously complex in English, but please be careful. Make sure your sentences make sense, and that they mean what you want them to mean.

7.3 Word Order

Standard word order is the most common sentence pattern in English. The subject comes before the verb.

Subject Verb: That book was heavy.

With inverted word order, the main verb or an auxiliary verb comes before the subject. The most common use of inverted word order in English is in forming direct questions.

7.3.1 Negatives: When you use negatives such as never, hardly ever, seldom, rarely, not only, or nor, a clause uses inverted order. These sentence pairs show the differences, first in standard order and then in inverted order.

I have never seen a more exciting movie. [Standard order]
Never have I seen a more exciting movie. [Inverted order]

She is not only a talented artist but also an excellent musician.

Not only is she a talented artist, but she is also an excellent musician.

How can I understand the placement of adjectives? Adjectives modify—describe or limit—nouns, pronouns, and word groups that function as nouns. In English, an adjective comes directly before the noun it describes. However, when more than one adjective describes the same noun, several sequences may be possible

Word order for more than one adjective:

1. Determiners, if any: a, an, the, my, your, this, that, these, those, and so on.
2. Expressions of order, including ordinal numbers, if any: first, second, third, next, last, final, and so on.
3. Expressions of quantity, including cardinal (counting) numbers, if any: one, two, few, each, every, some, and so on.
4. Adjectives of judgment or opinion, if any: pretty, happy, ugly, sad, interesting, boring, and so on.
5. Adjectives of size or shape, if any: big, small, short, round, square, and so on.
6. Adjectives of age or condition, if any: new, young, broken, dirty, shiny, and so on.
7. Adjectives of colour, if any: red, green, blue, and so on.
8. Adjectives that can also be used as nouns, if any: French, Protestant, metal, cotton, and so on.

How can I understand the placement of adverbs? Adverbs modify—describe or limit—verbs, adjectives, other adverbs, or entire sentences. Adverbs may be positioned first, in the middle, or last in clauses.

Below are given some basic guidelines and examples of usage. One should, however, be aware that there may be several options, depending on what the speaker wants to put emphasis on.

7.3.2 Use of Adverbs: Adverbs used in one, two or all three positions: beginning, middle, and end.

Adverbs Used Mostly in Mid-Position:

- Frequency: always, ever, hardly ever, never, often, rarely, seldom.
- Degree: almost, hardly, nearly, quite, scarcely.
- Probability: certainly, definitely, probably.
- Time: just.
- Examples: He has never attended an international conference. I quite understand what you mean.

Adverbs Used Mostly in Front or Mid-position:

- Frequency/time: sometimes, usually; eventually, finally.
- Examples: I sometimes work till late at night. Sometimes, I work till late at night.

Adverbs Used Mostly in Mid- or End-position:

- Frequency: constantly, continuously, regularly.
- Degree: completely, entirely, greatly.
- Time: already, lately, recently.
- Examples: The temperature was constantly rising. The temperature was rising constantly. I completely agree with you. I agree with you completely.

Adverbs Used Mostly in End- or Front-position:

- Place: above, here, there, at home, upstairs.
- Time/frequency: in January, last year; as a rule, from time to time, once.
- Probability: maybe, perhaps.
- Notes: With adverbs of place, time and frequency, the end position is more common; the front position is used to give importance or draw attention to the adverb.
- Examples: You will find a more detailed description

below. Below you will find a more detailed description. With maybe and perhaps, the front position is more common.

- Examples: Perhaps, you should ask him for help.

Adverbs Used in Any of the Three Positions:

- Manner: briefly, carefully, easily, quickly, slowly.
- Time/frequency: now, soon, immediately, suddenly, occasionally.
- Aspect: economically, financially, logically, scientifically, technically.
- Probability: apparently, certainly, clearly, evidently, obviously.

Adverbs Used Mostly in Front-position:

- Comment/opinion: admittedly, evidently, hopefully, naturally, surprisingly.
- Sentence linkers: however, consequently, as a result, nevertheless.
- Examples: Surprisingly, the experiment did not fail. He was evidently nervous.

7.3.3 Position of Adverbs of Manner, Place, and Time in One Sentence:

Normal position: He explained that problem thoroughly at the seminar last week.

The position can be changed in order to:

- emphasize/draw attention to one adverb: Last year I did not participate in that conference.
- avoid putting the longest adverb in the middle: I lived quite happily for one year in one of the remotest places in the world.
- avoid placing too many adverbs in the end position: In the mountains it is dangerous to drive fast in winters.

7.4 Words in Collocation

Collocation is a way in which some words are often used together, and sound natural together. This also refers to restrictions on how words may be used together, such as which verbs and nouns can be used together, and which prepositions and verbs can be used together. For example, we often say heavy rain, or light rain, instead of strong rain or mild rain, heavy goes well with rain, whereas strong does not. This sort of language behaviour is called collocation. There are many cases in English when it is difficult to know which words go well with the word you want to use, because there are no clear rules. Some words just sound right together, while others do not. So, students of English have to make a special effort to learn them because they are often difficult to guess.

Learning collocations is an important part of learning the vocabulary of a language. Some collocations are fixed, or very strong, for example take a photo, where no word other than take collocates with photo to give the same meaning. Some collocations are more open, where several different words may be used to give a similar meaning, for example keep to/stick to the rules. Here are some more examples of collocations.

7.4.1 Why Learn Collocations? Learning collocations is a good idea because they can:

- Give you the most natural way to say something: smoking is strictly forbidden is more natural than smoking is strongly forbidden.
- Give you alternative ways of saying something, which may be more colourful/expressive or more precise: instead of repeating "it was very cold and very dark", we can say "it was bitterly cold and pitch dark.
- Improve your style of writing: instead of saying poverty causes crime, you can say poverty breeds crime; instead of saying a big meal you can say a substantial meal. You may not need or want to use these in informal conversations, but in writing they can give your text better variety and make it read better. This book includes notes about formality wherever the collocations are especially formal or informal.

7.4.2 Learning Collocations: Learning collocations is not so different from learning any vocabulary item. The key things are to:

- Regularly revise what you want to learn.
- Practice using what you want to learn in contexts that are meaningful for you personally.
- Learn collocations in groups to help you fix them in your memory. You might group together collocations relating to the same topic. Or you might group collocations based on the same word.

However, a good learner's dictionary will give you information on collocations. Sometimes the information is highlighted in some special way. In other cases, the examples used in the dictionary include the most common collocations.

7.4.3 Verbs that Collocate with Nouns: When you use a noun in a sentence, you need to know which verbs go well with it. Learners often make mistakes with these verbs. For example:

- Instead of saying do a bath; you say take a bath.
- Instead of do an effort; you say make an effort.
- Instead of do a crime; you say commit a crime.
- Instead of say a joke, you say tell a joke, make a joke, or crack a joke

7.4.4 Adverbs that Collocate with Adjectives: For example, there are a number of intensifying adverbs that can be used instead of very or extremely with adjectives.

Often it is difficult to predict which adverb will be used with a particular adjective. Some adverbs occur quite often before some adjectives, e.g. perfectly normal (same as very normal) and grossly misleading (same as very...).

Examples:

- **Bitterly** ashamed, disappointed, resent, criticize, regret, cold; NOT bitterly successful.
- **Highly** accomplished, qualified, probable, praised, paid, placed, priced, pleased, interesting, controversial, unusual, competitive, profitable, effective, recommended; NOT highly divided, grateful.
- **Deeply** divided, grateful, unpopular, offended, ashamed,

concerned, shocked, committed, moved, affected, impressed, religious, hurt, grateful, touched; NOT deeply developed.

- **Utterly** ridiculous, wrong, impossible, stupid, devastated, miserable.
- **Strongly** oppose, influence, believe, deny, recommend, condemn, suggest, feel, argue.
- **Heavily** punished, drunk, loaded.
- **Seriously** ill, injured, worried.
- **Thoroughly** lazy, selfish, examine, changed, misleading.
- **Extremely** busy, tired, hard, glad, hot, cold.

7.4.5 Adjectives that Collocate with Nouns: When you want to describe a noun, there is often a range of adjectives you can use, e.g. you can say a strong, real, or distinct possibility when something is very possible, or a remote or faint possibility if something is not very likely.

Examples:

- **Bad** boy, weather, news, smell, name, cold, time, health.
- **Clean** air, shirt.
- **Clear** water, sky, light.
- **Deep** well, wound, sleep.
- **Great** man, war, care, joy.
- **Poor** man, health, soil.
- **Strong** animal, pillar, will, belief, smell, tea, wind.

7.4.6 Collocation of Some Verbs Used Everyday:

Make

- Make arrangements for
- Make a change/changes
- Make a choice.
- Make a comment/comments
- Make a contribution to
- Make a decision
- Make an effort
- Make an excuse
- Make friends

- Make an improvement
- Make a mistake
- Make a phone calf
- Make progress

Do

- Do your best
- Do damage
- Do an experiment
- Do exercises
- Do someone a good turn/do someone a favour
- Do harm
- Do your hair
- Do your homework
- Do the ironing/shopping/washing, etc.
- Do some work?

Have

- Have an accident
- Have an argument/a row
- Have a break
- Have a conversation/chat
- Have difficulty
- Have a dream/nightmare
- Have an experience
- Have a feeling have fun/a good time
- Have a look have a party
- Have a problem/problems
- Have a try/go

Pay

- Pay attention
- Pay a compliment
- Pay your (last) respects
- Pay tribute [formal]

7.5 Verb, Tense and Active versus Passive Voice

Social sciences and humanities normally use present tense:

"I analyze"; "This paper examines" etc. Conversely, past tense is usually used only in technical or scientific papers to describe experiments performed and results found: "We placed the sample", "the test proved" etc. This is a general rule, but whichever verb tense one prefers, stick with it and be consistent in writing.

Different academic disciplines, and different instructors within those disciplines, have varying attitudes to the use of the personal pronoun. Even though the passive voice is useful under certain circumstances, it is often actually better to use the active voice instead.

However, in academic and scholarly writing, there are legitimate reasons for authors to use the passive voice. Authors may wish to emphasize objectivity in their works. They may wish to focus on the study, process, instrument, or project under discussion rather than on the researcher or other individuals performing the work. They may also need to use the passive voice to eliminate anthropomorphism.

Anthropomorphism is the attribution of human behaviour and motivation to non-living or non-human things. We must be careful to avoid anthropomorphism, which appears most frequently in statements such as the following:

- **Incorrect:** The study proved that girls outperform boys in spelling.
- **Correct:** The study showed that girls outperform boys in spelling.
- **Correct:** The study indicated that girls outperform boys in spelling.
- **Correct:** The researchers found that girls outperform boys in spelling.
- **Incorrect**: The test found that 2 out of 3 individuals hate paying taxes.
- **Correct:** The test indicated that 2 out of 3 individuals hate paying taxes.
- **Correct:** Researchers found that 2 out of 3 individuals hate paying taxes.

In both the cases, the subjects of the sentence cannot physically do the actions indicated by the verbs: A study or a test cannot prove or demonstrate; only humans can engage in such actions. Studies or tests may show, indicate, or reveal. Anthropomorphism becomes more of a problem because of the preferences for using active voice and for not referencing the author of an article or dissertation.

In using the passive voice, authors must be cognizant of the potential problems with such constructions. Passive constructions may be more difficult for readers to follow, especially if the sentences contain several descriptive phrases or subordinate clauses. Such sentences are also often awkward or wordy.

8

Spelling Rules

Error free writing requires more than just using good grammar. You must also use correct mechanics of writing in your documents. The mechanics of writing specifies the established conventions for words that you use in your documentation. Grammar reflects the forms of words and their relationships within a sentence. For instance, if you put an apostrophe in a plural word ("create two file's"), you have made a mistake in the mechanics of writing, not grammar. In academic writing, one should be careful about the many of the errors found in student assignments which are usually straightforward, however. Students may be criticised, or even lose marks, because they have neglected some basic rules. Effective academic writing requires good grammar, spelling, and punctuation. Following things should be in order to make a text well-written that will get due credit from the readers.

Spelling is important for exactly the same reason that grammar and punctuation are important for. Poor spelling makes for poor communication. Academic writing requires a high degree of accuracy, and this is reflected in the quality of writing. Sloppy spelling gives the impression that you do not care about the assignment.

English spelling is notoriously whimsical and inconsistent. Spelling conventions have grown up over centuries as the result of the mixing of different languages (French, German, Latin, etc.) as well as different social fashions (for example, many of the differences between spelling in British English and American English can be traced to different social fashions).

As a general rule, written assignments should be properly written so as to effectively convey the intended meanings of the work. Hence, students are asked to pay attention to the language used, as the level of coherence in one's work can greatly influence the final grade for a written assignment. In other words, if the reader cannot understand what the student is saying, then his/her point will not be made. Therefore, to develop one's language skills and to help one avoid the most common spelling mistakes in English, there are several sources (in libraries and on the internet) that one can access. For example, the British Council grammar website which thoroughly explains the common areas of English grammar and where you could even test your proficiency level.

8.1 Syllables

Breaking a word down into syllables means you break a word down into little spoken chunks and each chunk is called a syllable. Each chunk usually has a vowel or vowel sound in it and different bits can be stressed: qua/li/fi/ca/tion, be/gin, swim/ming.

Syllable stress is also important to know but do not worry if syllables and stress is hard for you to figure out. Use your visual memory and words within words to help instead.

Stress on first syllable: CAREful

Second syllable stress: voCABulary

Last syllable stress: be'GIN, for'GET, pre'FER.

Adding 'es' to the end of words makes plurals and third person verbs:

- Ass–asses
- Atlas–atlases
- Bench–benches
- Box–boxes
- Bunch–bunches
- Bus–buses
- Bush–bushes
- Buzz–buzzes
- Carcass–carcasses
- Census–censuses

- Church–churches
- Crash–crashes
- Cross–crosses
- Crush–crushes
- Dash–dashes
- Fix–fixes
- Fizz–fizzes
- Flex–flexes
- Flush–flushes
- Fox–foxes
- Gas–gases
- Harness–harnesses
- Hunch–hunches
- Lunch–lunches
- Mix–mixes
- Pass–passes
- Porch–porches
- Rush–rushes
- Varnish–varnishes
- Whizz–whizzes
- Wish–wishes

When a word ends in 'se' or 'ze' we just add 's':

- Advise–advises
- Amaze–amazes
- Blaze–blazes
- Surprise–surprises

Words ending with a vowel + O, we always add 's':

- Audio–audios
- Cameo–cameos
- Cuckoo–cuckoos
- Kangaroo–kangaroos
- Patio-patios
- Radio–radios
- Ratio–ratios

- Stereo–stereos
- Studio–studios
- Tattoo–tattoos
- Video–videos
- Zoo–zoos

We add 'es' to the following words:

- Domino–dominoes
- Echo–echoes
- Embargo–embargoes
- Hero–heroes
- Mosquito–mosquitoes
- Potato–potatoes
- Tomato–tomatoes
- Torpedo–torpedoes
- Veto–vetoes

We have some words ending in 'O' that can be spelled with either 's' or 'es':

- Banjo–banjos or banjoes
- Buffalo–buffalo or buffaloes
- Cargo–cargos or cargoes
- Flamingo–flamingos or flamingoes
- Fresco–frescos or frescoes
- Ghetto–ghettos or ghettoes
- Halo–halos or haloes
- Mango–mangos or mangoes
- Memento–mementos or mementoes
- Motto–mottos or mottoes
- Tornado–tornados or tornadoes
- Tuxedo–tuxedos or tuxedoes
- Volcano–volcanos or volcanoes

Sometimes we add an 's' to words:

- Boy–boys
- Journey–journeys
- Tray–trays

Sometimes we change the 'y' to 'ies':

- Country–countries
- Cry–cries
- Party–parties

Most words ending in ‘f’ or ‘fe’ change their plurals to ‘ves’:

- Calf–calves
- Half–halves
- Knife–knives
- Leaf–leaves
- Life–lives
- Loaf–loaves
- Self–selves
- Shelf–shelves
- Thief–thieves
- Wife–wives
- Yourself–yourselves

For words ending in ‘ff’ you just add ‘s’ to make the plural:

- Bailiff–bailiffs
- Bluff–bluffs
- Cliff–cliffs
- Gaff–gaffs
- Scoff–scoffs
- Scuff–scuffs
- Sheriff–sheriffs
- Sniff–sniffs
- Tariff–tariffs
- Tuff–tuffs
- Whiff–whiffs

9

British English and American English

9.1 British and American Spelling

British and American spellings differ in several ways. The differences often come about because British English has tended to keep the spelling of words it has absorbed from other languages (e.g. French, Latin, Greek), while American English has adapted the spelling to reflect the way that the words actually sound when they are spoken. In most subjects, you are expected to consistently use British English (BrE) spellings. Even if you are allowed to use American English (AmE) spellings, it is important to stick to one style throughout your writing. Here is a list of the main ways in which British and American spellings differ.

Words ending with 're':

BrE words ending with 're' often end with 'er' in AmE:

- **British:** centre, metre, litre, theatre, calibre.
- **American:** center, meter, liter, theater, caliber.

Words ending with 'our':

BrE words ending with 'our' usually end with 'or' in AmE:

- **British:** colour, humour, neighbour, rumour, honour, behaviour, favour.
- **American:** color, humor, neighbor, rumor, behavior, favour.

Words ending with 'ise' or 'ize':

BrE verbs that can be spelled with either 'ise' or 'ize' at the end always end with 'ize' in AmE:

- **British:** apologize or apologise, organize or organize, recognize or recognize.
- **American:** apologize, organize, recognize.

Words ending with 'yse':

BrE verbs ending with 'yse' always end with 'yze' in AmE:

- **British:** analyse, paralyse, catalyse.

- **American:** analyze, paralyze, catalyze.

Words ending with 'ae' or 'oe':

BrE words spelled with the double vowels 'ae' or 'oe' are spelled with 'e' only in AmE:

- **British:** oestrogen, paediatric.
- **American:** estrogen, pediatric.

Words ending with 'ence':

BrE nouns ending with 'ence' sometimes end with 'ense' in AmE:

- **British:** defence, offence, licence.
- **American:** defense, offense, license.

Words ending with 'ogue':

BrE nouns ending with 'ogue' end with either 'og' or 'ogue' in AmE:

- **British:** analogue, dialogue, catalogue.
- **American:** analog or analogue, dialog or dialogue, catalog or catalogue.

9.2 Different Terms to Describe the Same Thing

Apart from spellings, there are also many cases in which the two varieties of English use different terms to describe the same thing (Table 9.1).

Table 9.1: Different Terms to Describe the Same Things

British English	American English
Accommodation	Accommodations
Action replay	Instant replay
Aerofoil	Airfoil
Aeroplane	Airplane
Agony aunt	Advice columnist
Allen key	Allen wrench
Aluminium	Aluminum
Aniseed	Anise
Anti-clockwise	Counter-clockwise
Articulated lorry	Tractor-trailer
Asymmetric bars	Uneven bars

Aubergine	Eggplant
Baking tray	Cookie sheet
Bank holiday	Legal holiday
Beetroot	Beet(s)
Biscuit	Cookie; cracker
Black economy	Underground economy
Blanket bath	Sponge bath
Block of flats	Apartment building
Boiler suit	Coveralls
Bonnet (*of a car*)	Hood
Boob tube	Tube top
Boot (*of a car*)	Trunk
Bottom drawer	Hope chest
Bowls	Lawn bowling
Braces	Suspenders
Brawn (*the food*)	Headcheese
Breakdown van	Tow truck
Breeze block	Cinder block
Bridging loan	Bridge loan
Bum bag	Fanny pack
Candy floss	Cotton candy
Car park	Parking lot
Casualty	Emergency room
Catapult	Slingshot
Central reservation	Median strip
Chemist	Drugstore
Chips	French fries
Cinema	Movie theater; the movies
Cling film	Plastic wrap
Common seal	Harbor seal
Consumer durables	Durable goods
Corn flour	Cornstarch
Cos	Romaine
Cot	Crib
Cot death	Crib death
Cotton bud	Cotton swab
Cotton wool	Absorbent cotton
Council estate	(Housing) project

Courgette	Zucchini
Court card	Face card
Crash barrier	Guardrail
Crisps	Chips; potato chips
Crocodile clip	Alligator clip
Cross-ply	Bias-ply
Crotchet (*music*)	Quarter note
Current account	Checking account
Danger money	Hazard pay
Demister (*in a car*)	Defroster
Dialing tone	Dial tone
Diamante	Rhinestone
Double cream	Heavy cream
Draughts (*game*)	Checkers
Drawing pin	Thumbtack
Dressing gown	Robe; bathrobe
Drink-driving	Drunk driving
Drinks cupboard	Liquor cabinet
Drinks party	Cocktail party
Driving licence	Driver's license
Dual carriageway	Divided highway
Dummy (*for a baby*)	Pacifier
Dust sheet	Drop cloth
Dustbin	Garbage can
Earth (*electrical*)	Ground
Engaged (*of a phone*)	Busy
Estate agent	Real estate agent, realtor
Estate car	Station wagon
Ex-directory	Unlisted
Faith school	Parochial school
Financial year	Fiscal year
Fire brigade/service	Fire company/department
First floor	Second floor
Fish finger	Fish stick
Fitted carpet	Wall-to-wall carpeting
Flannel	Washcloth
Flat	Apartment
Flexitime	Flextime

Flick knife	Switchblade
Flyover	Overpass
Football	Soccer
Footway	Sidewalk
Fringe (*hair*)	Bangs
Full stop (*punctuation)*	Period
Garden	Yard; lawn
Gearing (*finance*)	Leverage
Gear lever	Gearshift
Goods train	Freight train
Greaseproof paper	Wax paper/waxed paper
Green fingers	Green thumb
Grill (*noun*)	Broiler
Grill (*verb*)	Broil
Ground floor	First floor
Grounds man	Groundskeeper
Hair slide	Barrette
Hat stand	Hat rack
Hen night	Bachelorette party
Hire purchase	Installment plan
Hoarding	Billboard
Hob	Stovetop
Hold all	Carryall
Holiday	Vacation
Holidaymaker	Vacationer
Homely	Homey
Hosepipe	(Garden) hose
In hospital	In the hospital
Hot flush	Hot flash
Housing estate	Housing development
Hundreds and thousands	Sprinkles *(for ice cream)*
Ice lolly	Popsicle (*trademark*)
Icing sugar	Confectioners' sugar
Indicator (*in a car*)	Turn signal
Inside leg	Inseam
Jelly babies	Jelly beans
Joe Bloggs	Joe Blow
Joe Public	John Q. Public

Jumble sale	Rummage sale
Jump lead	Jumper cable
Jumper	Sweater
Junior school	Elementary school
Kennel	Doghouse
Ladybird	Ladybug
A lettuce	A head of lettuce
Level crossing	Grade crossing
Lift	Elevator
Lolly	Lollipop
Lollipop lady (or man)	Crossing guard
Loose cover	Slipcover
Lorry	Truck
Loudhailer	Bullhorn
Low loader	Flatbed truck
Lucky dip	Grab bag
Luggage van	Baggage car
Maize	Corn
Mange tout	Snow pea
Market garden	Truck farm
Marshalling yard	Railroad yard
Maths	Math
Metalled road	Paved road
Milometer	Odometer
Minim *(music)*	Half note
Mobile phone	Cell phone
Monkey tricks	Monkeyshines
Motorway	Expressway; highway
Mum/mummy	Mom/mommy
Nappy	Diaper
Needle cord	Pinwale
Newsreader	Newscaster
Noughts crosses	Tic-tac-toe
Number plate	License plate
Off-licence liquor	Store; package store
Opencast mining	Open-pit mining
Ordinary share	Common stock
Oven glove	Oven mitt

Paddling pool	Wading pool
Paracetamol	Acetaminophen
Parting (*in hair*)	Part
Patience	Solitaire
Pavement	Sidewalk
Pay packet	Pay envelope
Pedestrian crossing	Crosswalk
Peg	Clothespin
Pelmet	Valance
Petrol	Gas; gasoline
Physiotherapy	Physical therapy
Pinafore dress	Jumper
Plain chocolate	Dark chocolate
Plain flour	All-purpose flour
Polo neck	Turtleneck
Positive discrimination	Reverse discrimination
Postal vote	Sbsentee ballot
Post-box	Mail-box
Postcode	Zip code
Potato crisp	Potato chip
Power point	Electrical outlet
Pram	Baby carriage; stroller
Press stud	Snap
Press-up	Push-up
Private soldier	GI
Public school	Private school
Public transport	Public transportation
Punch bag	Punching bag
Pushchair	Stroller
Pylon	Utility pole
Quantity surveyor	Estimator
Quaver (*music*)	Eighth note
Queue	Line
Racing car	Race car
Railway	Railroad
Real tennis	Court tennis
Recorded delivery	Certified mail
Registration plate	License plate

Remould (*tyre*)	Retread
Reverse the charges	Call collect
Reversing lights	Back-up lights
Right-angled triangle	Right triangle
Ring road	Beltway
Roundabout *(at a fair)*	Carousel
Roundabout (*in road)*	Traffic circle
Rowing boat	Rowboat
Sailing boat	Sailboat
Saloon (*car)*	Sedan
Sandpit	Sandbox
Sandwich cake	Layer cake
Sanitary towel	Sanitary napkin
Self-raising flour	Self-rising flour
Semibreve (*music)*	Whole note
Semitone *(music)*	Half step
Share option	Stock option
Shopping trolley	Shopping cart
Show house/home	Model home
Silencer (*on a car*)	Muffler
Silverside	Rump roast
Skeleton in the cupboard	Skeleton in the closet
Skimmed milk	Skim milk
Skipping rope	Jump rope
Skirting board	Baseboard
Sledge	Sled
Sleeper	Railroad tie
Sleeping partner	Silent partner
Slowcoach	Slowpoke
Snakes and ladders	Chutes and ladders
Solicitor	Lawyer
Soya/soyabean	Soy/soybean
Splash back	Back splash
Spring onion	Scallion
Stag night	Bachelor party
Stanley knife	Utility knife
St .rter	Appetizer
State school	Public school

Storm in a teacup	Tempest in a teapot
Surtitle	Supertitle
Swede	Rutabaga
Sweet	Candy
Takeaway (*food*)	Takeout; to go
Taxi rank	Taxi stand
Tea towel	Dish towel
Terrace house	Row house
Tick	Check mark
Ticket touts	Scalper
Timber	Lumber
Titbit	Tidbit
Toffee apple	Candy apple or caramel apple
Touch wood	Knock on wood
Trade union	Labor union
Trading estate	Industrial park
Trainers	Sneakers
Transport cafe	Truck stop
Trolley	Shopping cart
Twelve-bore	Twelve-gauge
Underground	Subway
Vacuum flask	Thermos bottle
Verge (*of a road*)	Shoulder
Vest	Undershirt
Veterinary surgeon	Veterinarian
Wagon (*on a train*)	Car
Waistcoat	Vest
Walking frame	Walker
Wardrobe	Closet
Water ice	Italian ice
Weatherboard	Clapboard
White coffee	Coffee with cream
White spirit	Mineral spirits
Whole meal bread	Whole-wheat bread
Windcheater	Windbreaker
Windscreen	Windshield
Wing (*of a car*)	Fender
Worktop	Countertop

Zebra crossing	Crosswalk
Zed (*letter Z*)	Zee
Zip	Zipper

10

Punctuation

The word punctuation is derived from Latin word *punctum* which means 'bring to a point'. Punctuation marks have a great importance in every language. Using correct punctuation is important because punctuation conveys meaning just as words do. Consider these two sentences:

Eat children.

Eat, children.

Both sentences are commands, but the first sentence would be correct only in a society of cannibals. So it is important to learn and practice the rules of punctuation until someone is confident about using them correctly.

10.1 Capitalization

The chief reason to capitalize a word is that the word is proper, not because the word has greater status than other words. A proper noun identifies a specific member of a class. A common noun, on the other hand, denotes either the whole class or any random member of the class. For example, King Henry VIII (a particular member of a class) was a king of England (the class itself).

10.1.1 What to Capitalize: Capitalize the following items:

- First word in a sentence.
- First person pronoun.
- Proper nouns.
- Days of the week.
- Months of the year.
- Public holidays.
- Nationalities.
- Languages.

- Geographical locations.

10.1.2 What Not to Capitalize: Do not capitalize the following items:

- The word "page" when followed by a number. Thus, refer to page 45.
- The spelled-out words in most acronyms and abbreviations. Thus, field-replaceable unit (FRU); direct memory access (DMA).

10.2 Full Stop

Full stop represents the greatest pause and separation; it is used at the end of a complete sentence, except interrogative and exclamatory sentences.

- I am a teacher.
- Shut the door.
- It is also used to mark certain abbreviation: M.L.A., M.A.

10.3 Commas

Commas are sometimes troublesome to learners of English language because they are used differently in other languages. There are many comma rules in English, but you may remember them more easily if you realize that they can be organized into just four main groups: introducers, coordinators, inserters, and tags. Each group of commas relates to independent clauses in a particular way, except the coordinator group. Coordinator commas link not just independent clauses but any coordinate (equal) elements in a sentence.

Study the examples for each comma group, and notice the kind of elements that can be introducers, coordinators, inserters, and tags.

10.3.1 Introducer Commas: An introducer comma follows any element that comes in front of the first independent clause in a sentence.

- After 16 years of smoking, it is not easy to quit. (Phrase)
- Therefore, I plan to quit smoking. (Word)

- Because I have a chronic cough, my doctor recommended that I quit immediately. (Dependent Clause)
- "Stop smoking today", she advised. (Direct Quotation)

10.3.2 Co-ordinator Commas: Together with a co-ordinating conjunction, a comma links co-ordinate (equal) elements in a sentence.

- They were tired, so they went home early. (Independent Clauses)
- Cecille speaks English, Spanish, French, and Creole. (No comma with only two items)

10.3.3 Inserter Commas: An inserter comma is used before and after any element that is inserted into the middle of an independent clause.

- My uncle, however, refuses to quit smoking. (Word)
- My father, on the other hand, has never smoked. (Phrase)
- "I have tried to quit smoking a dozen times", she says, "but I can't". (Reporting Verb)

10.3.4 Tag Commas: A tag comma is used when adding certain elements to the end of a sentence.

- He appears to be in good health, however. (Word)
- He swims for an hour every day, for example. (Phrase)
- It is not logical, is it? (Tag Question)
- He laughs as he says, "I will outlive all of you". (Direct Quotation)

10.4 Semicolon (;)

It is a midway between a full stop and a comma that separates two contrasting parts of a sentence. It is used in the following situations:

It is used to separate two contrasting parts of a sentence.

- Sambit wanted to go; I did not.
- To err is human; to forgive is divine.

It is used to join two sentence structures not connected by and, but, for, and or.

- We'll have to hurry; it's almost five o' clock.

10.5 Colon (:)

The colon mark is most commonly used as a longer pause than the semicolon or a comma. It is used in the following situations:

It introduces a quotation:

- All of us know the proverb: "Necessity is the mother of invention".

It introduces lists:

- I have a taste for different food: Chinese, Continental, and Indian.

It separates two ideas:

- Man proposes: God disposes.

It is used between the hour and the minutes:

- 5:15 P.M.

10.6 Apostrophe (')

It is used to make a possessive case:

- Boy's hostel.
- President's house.

It is used for contracted forms:

- Don't, Let's, I've, He's

It is used to form the plural of letters and figures:

- 4's, 6's

10.7 Inverted Commas/Quotation Marks (" ")

Used to denote the exact words of a speaker:

- According to Aristotle, "Man is a rational animal".

If there is a quotation within a quotation, the internal quotation is closed with a single quotation, and the whole quotation is closed within a double quotation mark.

10.8 Dash (—)

It is used to indicate an abrupt stop or a change of thought.

- If my father was alive—but why think of the past?

It is used to collect stray thoughts.

- Family, friends, followers—all left him.

10.9 Hyphen (-)

The mark of hyphen is smaller than the dash, and is used to connect the parts of a compound word.

- Father-in-law, twenty-one, one-third.

10.10 Parentheses ( )

Parentheses normally stand for round brackets and generally used for in-text citations.

11

Common Errors in English

An error is distinguished from a mistake. Errors are a natural part of the learning process which the learners may make. Errors normally refer to those ill-formed constructions or deviation from Standard English usage which is not acceptable in the present day English It may occur in grammar, spelling or punctuation. All academic writing should be error free. Any piece of academic writing with errors creates a poor impression in the mind of the reader about the learner. Avoiding common errors ensures our speech or writing as clear, precise, comprehensible, and free from ambiguity. Errors related to spelling and punctuation have been dealt in previous chapters. The present chapter will focus on the other aspects of errors that we generally make.

11.1 Common Uncountable Nouns

Here are some common uncountable nouns that are often used incorrectly. Remember not to use a/an with them and do not make them plural:

Accommodation, absence, agriculture, capacity, comfort, courage, duty, education, evil, experience, existence, equipment, evidence, fruit, fun, failure, faith, fear, food, history, intelligence, joy, justice, permission, poverty, poetry, stationery, stuff, time, truth, water, wind, weather, youth, housework, trouble, following, advice, information, work, dozen, furniture, knowledge, machinery, money, progress, research, traffic, hair, baggage, luggage, homework, thunder, rain, snow

Note: Uncountable nouns can be used with certain determiners (e.g. *my, her, some, any, no, the, this, that*) and expressions of quantity (e.g. *a lot of, (a) little*).

They gave me **some information** about courses and scholarships and things.

She's been studying hard and has made **a lot of progress**.

Some uncountable nouns end in 's' and look as if they are plural. Do not put **a/an** with them, and make sure to use a singular verb with them.

Aerobics, athletics, acoustics, aeronautics, classics, cards, darts, diabetes, ethics, economics, electronics, genetics, gymnastics, innings, linguistics, logistics, mathematics, measles, mechanics, mumps, physics, politics, rabies, statistics, thermodynamics.

11.1.1 Plural Nouns: The following nouns are generally used in plural form:

Arrears, ashes, bounds, circumstances, conditions, damages, directions, earnings, expenses, findings, foundations, funds, marks, grounds, instructions, manners, minutes, orders, outskirts, proceedings, regards, relations, resources, respects, results, rights, savings, steps, vegetables, arms, headquarters, particulars, premises,

But there are several nouns that have no singular form and are always used in plural:

Annals, clothes, contents, congratulations, belongings, surroundings, ruins, thanks, whereabouts, trousers, summons, binoculars, jeans, pants, scissors, shorts, sunglasses, pyjamas, leggings, trunks, underpants, compasses, dividers, pincers, tweezers, riches, alms, caves, species, wages, premises, vegetables, tidings, troops,

Collective nouns refer to a group of people or things. One should not use **a/an** or **a number** in front of them when referring to a member or more than one member of that group.

Here is a list of some common collective nouns:

Army, aristocracy, audience, cattle, clergy, committee, community, council, company, crew, data, enemy, family, flock, gang, gentry, government, group, herd, infantry, jury, navy, nobility, media, panel, press, proletariat, public, staff, team.

11.1.2 More about Nouns: Some nouns that indicate money, weight, length, measure, number etc. when preceded by a numeral, remain unchanged in form. For example, year, pair, foot, metre, million, dozen, score, hundred, thousand etc.

Some nouns have one meaning in singular and another meaning in plural (Table 11.1).

Table 11.1: Singular and Plural Words with Different Meanings

Singular (normal meaning)	Plural (different meaning)
Wood	Woods (jungle)
Good	Goods (luggage)
Colour	Colours (flag)
Air	Airs (arrogant show)
Alphabet	Alphabets (language)
Ground	Grounds (enclosed land attached to house)
Force	Forces (soldiers)
Iron	Irons (fetters)

11.2 Choice between Competing Words

- **Able or capable?** Able and capable are both used to say that someone can do something. However, they are used with different patterns.
- **Accept or agree?** Do not say that you accept to do what someone suggests. You say that you agree to do it.
- **Air or Wind?** Air is what we breathe, and wind is what makes the leaves of the trees move.
- **Allow or permit?** *Allow* implies absence of opposition; *permit* implies approval or sanction.
- **Amount of or number of?** *Amount of* is usually used with uncountable nouns; *number of* is used with countable nouns.
- **Amount or number?** Do not use amount in front of plural countable nouns. Use number instead. Use amount in front of uncountable nouns.
- **Answer or reply?** We *answer* a question but we *reply* to a

charge or an objection.

- **Avoid or prevent?** *Avoid* is used to stay away from someone or something. *Prevent* is used to talk about allowing someone to do something.
- **Battle or fight?** *Battle* is a fight between two organized forces; *fight* means quarrel, act of fighting.
- **Beautiful or Handsome/Good-looking?** We usually say that a man is handsome or good-looking, and that a woman is beautiful, lovely, good looking or pretty.
- **Because or because of?** *Because* is a conjunction and is used before a clause. *Because of* is a preposition and is always used before a noun or noun phrase.
- **Because or since?** *Because* is used when a reason is involved; *since* is used when time or cause is involved.
- **Before or Ago?** We use *ago* in counting from the time of speaking to a point in the past; half an hour ago, three days ago, four months ago, five years ago, a long time ago. We use *before* in counting from a distant to a nearer point in the past. Napoleon died in 1821, he had lost the battle of Waterloo six years before.
- **Besides or also?** We use *besides* at the beginning of a clause to add a fact or reason that is stronger than what is said. *Also* is used to add extra information.
- **Borrow or Lend?** *To borrow* is to get something from someone, and *to lend* is to give something to someone.
- **Build up or build?** To talk about making something by putting materials together *build* is used. *Build up* is used to praise someone or something in a way which will influence people's opinion.
- **Cause of or Reason for?** *A cause* is that which produces a result; *a reason* is that which explains or justifies a result.
- **Celebrate or observe?** *Celebrate* means doing something enjoyable while *observe* means to obey or follow.
- **Centre or middle?** *Centre* is the point that is equidistant from the edge of a circle. *Middle* is the area equidistant from two sides: middle of the road, middle of the room,

middle of the page, etc.

- **Character or conduct?** Character denotes a man's real quality; conduct denotes that which a man does.
- **Childish or childlike?** *Childish* is selfish and irresponsible while the word *childlike* means simple and innocent.
- **Chronic or acute?** The word *chronic* means for a long time while the word *acute* means severe.
- **Common or ordinary?** *Common* means belonging, equally to, or shared by two or more people. *Ordinary* means not specially or different in anyway, not unusually.
- **Contrary or opposite?** *Contrary* is diametrically or mutually opposed; *opposite* is diametrically different.
- **Cost or Price?** *Price* is the amount of money paid by the customer. *Cost* is the amount paid by the shopkeeper. We can say, 'How much does it cost'?
- **Discover or Invent?** *To discover* is to find that which existed before but was unknown, and *to invent* is to create that which didn't exist before
- **Discover or invent?** *To discover* means to find out a thing that existed before, but was not known; *to invent* means to create or find out what did not exist before.
- **Doubt or suspect?** *Doubt* means to feel uncertain or question the truth of; *suspect* means to imagine something is true.
- **Each or Every?** Use *each* for one of two or more things. Never use *every* for two, but always for more than two things, taken as a group each is more individual and specific, but every is a more emphatic word. Note each and every are always singular: Each (or every) one of the twenty boys has a book.
- **Emerge or immerse?** *Emerge* means to come out, where as *immerse* means to dip in liquid.
- **Empty or vacant?** The word *empty* means containing nothing while the word *vacant* means a place or space not being used or occupied at the moment.

- **Far or away?** *Far* is mainly used in questions and negative sentences to talk in general distance in place or time. *Away* is used to talk about specific distance.
- **Farther or Further?** Use *further* to mean both greater distance and more of something. We only use *farther* for distances.
- **Fetch or bring?** *Fetch* means 'to go, get and bring'; *bring* means 'to come taking something with oneself'.
- **Finish or end?** The word *finish* means to bring something to an end while *end* means cause something to come to an end.
- **Godly or Godlike?** *Godly* means pious; *Godlike* means like God.
- **Ground or floor?** *The floor* is the part of the room on which we walk. *The ground* is outside the house.
- **High or tall?** We generally use *tall* with people, and it is the opposite of short. Use *high* when referring to trees, buildings, or mountains, and it is the opposite of low.
- **Historic or historical?** *Historic* means significance to history whereas *historical* is based on a period of history.
- **Hope or expect?** *Hope* refers to good expectations, wishes, but *expect* means that a thing is probable.
- **House or home?** Take care not to say my house, his house, or your house when you should say home. *A house* is any building used for dwelling in, and *home* is the particular house in which someone is living.
- **In future or in the future?** *In future* is used to talk about what will happen starting from now. To talk about what will happen in a period of time that is to come, *in the future* is used.
- **Later or latter?** *Later* refers to a time in future; *latter* refers to the second of the two.
- **Less or Fewer?** *Less* denotes amount, quantity, value, or degree, *fewer* denotes number. We may have less water, less food, less money, less education, but fewer books, fewer letters, fewer friends.

- **Made from or Made of?** We usually use *of* when you can still recognise the original material. We use *from* when the original material is unrecognisable. In most cases either is possible.
- **Many or Much?** Use *many* with plural nouns like many books or many boys. Use *much* with uncountable nouns such as, much water or much bread.
- **No or Not?** We use *no* meaning not as an adjective to qualify the noun. If the noun is already qualified by an adjective, like any, much, enough, we must use the adverb *not*. Note: We only use no as an adverb before a comparative: have no more to say.
- **On the contrary or in contrast?** Use *on the contrary* to show that you think or feel the opposite of what has just been said. If we are comparing two things and the second thing is very different to the first use *in contrast*.
- **Online or on line?** *Online* is related to computer technology; *on line* is used in relation to telephone calls.
- **Possible or probable?** *Possible* means something that can happen or that can be done. *Probable* means something that is likely to happen.
- **Presently or at present?** At present and presently are not synonymous. *At present* means now, *but presently* means soon: She will come back presently (= soon).
- **Rare or scarce?** *Rare* is applied to things which are seldom found. *Scarce* is applied to things which are in short supply, usually only temporarily.
- **Refuse or Deny?** *To refuse* means not to take what is offered or not to do what one is asked to do. *To deny* means to answer in the negative or to say that a statement isn't true.
- **Scarcely or rarely?** Scarcely isn't synonymous with rarely. *Rarely* means not often, *scarcely* means not quite.
- **Sick or ill?** To be *ill* means to be in bad health. To be *sick* means to vomit. We sometimes use sick idiomatically to mean feeling ill. *The smell made me sick.*

- **Speak or talk?** *Speak* means to utter words in an ordering voice not singing while *talk* means to say things, speak to give information, or discuss something.
- **Steal or rob?** The object of *steal* is the thing taken by the thief, such as money, a watch, a bicycle, etc., while the object of *rob* is the person or place from whom (or which) the thing is taken, such as a man, a house, or a bank.
- **Story or history?** *A story* is an account of events which may or may not be true. *History* is a systematic record of past events.
- **Travel or journey?** *Travel* is a verb, used to describe any type of movement from one place to another. *Journey* is the noun but we also use (take a) trip for having a short journey: We took a trip to the seaside last Sunday. We also use travelling as noun. We use a possessive pronoun with travels as an idiom: *Jenny is off on her travels again.*
- **Use or usage?** *Use* means utilize or the action of doing something; *usage* means practice or habitual use of something at a particular period of time.
- **Very or Too?** *Very* simply makes the adjective or adverb stronger. *Too* means more than enough, or so much that something else happens as a result.
- **Withhold or withstand?** *Withhold* means to keep back; *withstand* means to resist or oppose.

11.3 Tense Error

Some verbs are never or very rarely used in the progressive form. Many of them belong to certain categories, for example, verbs that relate to the senses and verbs that express belief and preference. Here is a list of common verbs that are not usually used in the progressive form:

Agree, be, believe, belong, contain, cost, depend, disagree, dislike, doubt, fit, hate, hear, imagine, include, involve, know, like, love, mean, need, owe, own, prefer, promise, realize, recognize, remember, seem, sell, sound, suppose, surprise, understand, want.

Adverbs such as "always, usually, often, and never" are normally used in present simple.

To say how long something has continued to the present time, we use 'for' plus a period of time, or 'since' plus a date or time in the past. Do not confuse 'for' with 'since'.

Examples:

I have been working since six o'clock this morning.

I have lived here since 2008.

We have known each other for over ten years.

When we talk about an event that started and finished in the past and we say exactly when it happened, we must use the past simple and not the present perfect. However, that with the perfect, we can use an adverb that shows how long a situation or event lasts or takes, such as "always or forever".

Examples:

I didn't have breakfast this morning.

I have always loved music.

11.4 Errors in Verb Patterns

11.4.1 Use of Verbs: The way in which a verb is used in a sentence is explained below.

The following list of common verbs is used with a **to+ infinitive** and rarely or never with an infinitive without 'to' or an **–ing** verb:

Afford, agree, aim, appear, arrange, ask, attempt, choose, claim, decide, demand, deserve, expect, fail, fight, forget, grow, help, hesitate, hope, intend, learn, manage, mean, need, offer, plan, prefer, pretend, promise, refuse, seem, tend, threaten, wait, want, wish.

The following list of common verbs is used with an **-ing** verb, and are rarely or never used with an infinitive:

Admit, appreciate, avoid, consider, delay, deny, describe, dislike, enjoy, fancy, finish, hate, imagine, keep, like, look forward to, love, mention.

Example: He kept asking me to help him.

Verbs such as like, hate, dislike, and love when used to say how we feel about an event or situation, need the word 'it' when they are followed by "when or if".

Example: I hate it when you laugh at me.

Suggest/recommend that...

Example: I suggest that you go to Delhi.

I recommend that you take the train ('want' is not followed by a 'that' clause).

Thinking of +ing verb:

Example: I am thinking of leaving home.

Wish + past tense:

Example: I wish I had passed.

Can see/hear/feel etc...

Example: I can hear an owl.

I can taste the garlic.

After some reporting verbs like reply, argue, deny, say, enquire, insist, do not mention the hearer.

Example: He replied me that he was helpless. (Incorrect)

He replied that he was helpless. (Correct)

The following list of verbs is used without prepositions before an object:

Answer, approach, accompany, ask, call, comprise, consult, discuss, describe, emphasize, investigating, joined, lacks, entered, escaped, married, mention, obey, remember, phone, resemble, reach, resign, order.

11.4.2 Using Reflexive Pronoun after Verbs: Use reflexive pronoun to talk about a situation where the same person is involved as both the subject and the object of an action.

Example: He taught himself to speak English.

He enjoyed himself at the concert.

11.4.3 Use of Passive Forms: The verbs 'let' and 'consist of' are never used in the passive form. The verb 'get' is not usually used in passive in formal English. Other verbs that are never or very rarely used in the passive are "have, resemble, and suit".

11.5 Concord (Agreement of Verb with Subject)

In English, subjects and verbs must agree in number (singular or plural) and person (first, second, or third). Singular subjects take singular verbs, and plural subjects take plural verbs.

Example: Bob is working as a camp counsellor this summer (The singular subject Bob agrees with the singular verb 'is').

Jake and John are competing in the state championship (The plural subject Jake and John agrees with the plural verb 'are').

11.5.1 Subjects and Verbs Separated by Words or Phrases: When words or phrases separate the subject and verb, the verb should agree with the subject, not with the words in the modifying phrase. To find the subject of the sentence, find the verb and ask Who? or What? is doing the action.

Example: The houses on Apple Street were built two years ago (What were built? Houses were built. The plural verb here agrees with the plural subject the houses, not the phrase on Apple Street).

11.5.2 Compound Subjects Joined by And: Compound subjects joined by **and** are usually treated as plural; therefore, they use plural verbs.

Example: Bob and Sarah are moving to Washington this summer (The plural subject Bob and Sarah agrees with plural verb 'are').

When the compound subject is joined by **and** but represents a single idea or person, the compound subject is treated as a unit and a singular verb is used.

Example: Ham and eggs is a popular breakfast dish (Ham and eggs refers to a single dish).

When a compound subject joined by **and** is preceded by **each** or **every**, a singular verb is used.

Example: Every student and teacher has to wear a uniform. (The singular verb **has** agrees with every, not student and teacher).

11.5.3 Compound Subjects Joined by Or: Compound subjects joined by **or** or by **either...or** or **neither...nor** may take singular or plural verbs.

When both subjects are singular, use a singular verb; if both subjects are plural, use a plural verb.

Examples: Either Sarah or Tom has the exam schedule (Both Sara and Tom are singular and agree with the singular verb 'has').

Neither snakes nor rats are considered good pets (snakes and rats are plural and agree with the plural verb 'are').

When one subject is singular and the other is plural, the verb agrees with the subject that is closest to it.

Examples: Either the cats or the dog is responsible for the mess (The singular subject dog is closest to the verb so the singular verb 'is' is used).

Either the teacher or the students are bringing the books (The plural subject students is closest to the verb so the plural verb 'are' is used).

11.5.4 Indefinite Pronouns as Subjects: A verb must agree in number with an indefinite pronoun (pronouns that do not refer to a particular person, thing, or group) subject. Some indefinite pronouns are singular and take singular verbs. Always singular: anybody, anyone, anything, each, either, everybody, everyone, everything, neither, no one, nobody, nothing, one, somebody, someone, and something.

Example: Everyone in the office is invited to the charity benefit (Everyone is always singular and agrees with the singular verb 'is').

Some indefinite pronouns are plural and take plural verbs. Always plural: both, few, fewer, many, other/others, and several.

Example: Several students are attending the history lecture (Several is always plural and agrees with the plural verb 'are').

Other indefinite pronouns can be either singular or plural depending on the noun they refer to. Either singular or plural:

all, any, half, more, most, no, none, and some.

Example: All of the food is bad (All of the food refers to a single unit so the singular verb 'is' is used). All of the cars are damaged (All of the cars refers to numerous cars so the plural verb 'are' is used).

11.5.5 Collective Nouns as Subjects: Collective nouns name a group or a collection of persons or things (family, union, group, committee).

When the collective noun refers to a group as a unit, a singular verb is used.

Example: The committee is meeting on Friday (The committee refers to a single group so the singular verb 'is' is used).

When the collective noun refers to the individuals or items that make up the group, a plural verb is used.

Example: The committee have met the requirements set by the board of directors (The committee refers to each individual member of the committee so the plural verb 'have' is used).

11.5.6 Singular Subject with Plural Forms of Nouns: Some nouns that end in –s, such as statistics, economics, and mathematics, act as singular subjects; therefore, they use singular verbs.

Example: Statistics is Jake's favourite subject (Statistics is used as a singular subject with a singular verb 'is').

However, when such a word has a plural meaning, use a plural verb.

Example: The researcher's statistics are the basis for his argument (Statistics is used as a plural subject with the plural verb 'are').

11.5.7 Inverted Subject-Verb Order: In inverted sentences, the subject follows the verb. The sentence may begin with a prepositional phrase, the words here or there, or the verb form of do. Even in this case, the subject and the verb must agree. If the sentence begins with a prepositional phrase, ask Who? or What?, is doing the action,

Example: In the centre of the mall stand four statues.

(What stands in the centre of the mall?; Four statues. The plural verb stand agrees with the plural subject four statues).

Here are the books that you ordered (The plural verb 'are' agrees with the plural subject books).

Do the employees consent to the terms in the contract? (The plural verb consent agrees with the plural subject employees).

11.5.8 With Linking Verbs: In sentences with linking verbs (verbs that link or join the subject with an adjective, a noun, or a pronoun), the verb agrees with the subject, not with the subject complement.

Example: Jake's favourite food is chocolate chip cookies (The singular verb 'is' agrees with the singular subject food).

Chocolate chip cookies are Jake's favourite food (The plural verb 'are' agrees with the plural subject chocolate chip cookies).

11.5.9 With Relative Pronouns: When using a relative pronoun (who, which, that, what, whatever, and whoever) to introduce a dependent clause, that verb in the clause should agree in number with the pronoun's antecedent (the word to which the pronoun refers).

Example: Jake is the only one who has a security pass (The singular verb 'has' agrees with the singular antecedent one).

11.5.10 More about Agreement: When a plural noun refers to some specific quantity or amount considered as a whole, singular verb is used.

Example: Sixty minutes is not enough to complete this work.

Fifty kilometres is a long distance.

When the adjectives like **much, less, little**, and **more** are used as nouns they must have a singular verb.

Example: A little learning is a dangerous thing.

When a sentence begins with the word there + the verb be, the subject follows the 'be' verb.

Examples:

There is a student in the hall (The verb 'is' is singular to agree with a student).

There are three students in the hall (The verb 'are' is plural to agree with three students).

There was no reason for his action.

There were many reasons for his success.

A prepositional phrase (a group of words beginning with a preposition such as: **of, with, in, at**, or **on** and ending with a noun or pronoun) can come between a subject and its verb. Prepositional phrases may come after a subject, but they are not part of the subject. You should mentally cross them out when you are deciding if the verb should be singular or plural.

Examples:

One (of my sisters) is a singer (The subject is one, not sisters.)

The color (of her eyes) changes when she is angry (The subject is color, not eyes.)

Six kinds (of rice) are available in the grocery store (The subject is kinds, not rice.)

A few words can be either singular or plural. In these cases, you must refer to the noun in the prepositional phrase.

Examples:

Some (of the money) was missing. (Singular)

Some (of the students) were missing. (Plural)

All (of my time) is spent in the library. (Singular)

All (of my brothers) are singers. (Plural)

Most (of the ice) was melted. (Singular)

Most (of the ice cubes) were melted. (Plural)

A lot (of the work) was too easy. (Singular)

A lot (of the people) were angry. (Plural)

None (of the fruit) is fresh. (Singular)

None (of the apples) are fresh. (Plural)

12

Redundancies

Conciseness is also a mark of good academic writing. To write effectively we should learn to write precisely and concisely, using only as many words as are necessary to convey what we want to say. Do not add words just to lengthen your essay or create fancy expressions. It is far more important to get our message across effectively.

In speech, we often use redundant words because listeners may not catch them the first time. However, we do not need redundancy in written texts because readers can backtrack and re-read what they have missed. In fact, redundant words in written texts are annoying and take up space. Redundancy occurs when a writer unnecessarily repeats something. Writers should avoid redundancy not only because it distracts and annoys readers but also because it adds unnecessary length to one's writing. Eliminating redundancy is a good way to revise our writing for concision, or the ability to make our point in as few words as needed. See the following examples:

There is a **more preferable** method to do this.

This is the **most unique** case we have yet seen.

If you prefer something, you like it more than something else; therefore, **more** is redundant. In the second case, **unique** means *one of its kind*, with no equal; so strictly speaking, you cannot have varying degrees of uniqueness.

Another area where redundancy occurs is in the use of prepositions. These are often the ones which appear with verbs but are actually not necessary (as given in parentheses).

Examples:

- Comprise (of)
- Emphasize (on)
- Stress (upon)

- Despite (of)
- Discuss (about)
- Request (for)

Following list of redundant words (given in parentheses) need to be avoided while writing an academic text:

(Absolutely) essential • (Absolutely) necessary • (Actual) facts • Advance (forward) • (Advance) planning • (Advance) preview • (Advance) reservations • (Advance) warning • Add (an additional) • Add (up) • (Added) bonus • (Affirmative) yes • (Aid and) abet • (All-time) record • Alternative (choice) • A.M. (in the morning) • (And) etc. • (Anonymous) stranger • (Annual) anniversary • (Armed) gunman • (Artificial) prosthesis • Ascend (up) • Ask (the question) • Assemble (together) • Attach (together) • ATM (machine) • Autobiography (of his or her own life).

Bald (-headed) • Balsa (wood) • (Basic) fundamentals • (Basic) necessities • Best (ever) • Biography (of his- or her-life) • Blend (together) • (Boat) marina • Bouquet (of flowers) Brief (in duration) • (Brief) moment • (Brief) summary • (Burning) embers.

Cacophony (of sound) • Cameo (appearance) • Cancel (out) • (Careful) scrutiny • Cash (money) • Cease (and desist) Circle (around) • Circulate (around) • Classify (into groups) (Close) proximity • (Closed) fist • Collaborate (together) • Combine (together) • Commute (back and forth) • Compete (with each other) • (Completely) annihilate • (Completely) destroyed • (Completely) eliminate • (Completely) engulfed • (Completely) filled • (Completely) surround • (Component) parts • Confer (together) • Connect (together) • Connect (up) Confused (state) • Consensus (of opinion) • (Constantly) maintained • Cooperate (together) • Could (possibly) • Crisis (situation) • Curative (process) • (Current) incumbent • (Current) trend.

Depreciate (in value) • Descend (down) • (Desirable) benefits • (Different) kinds • Disappear (from sight) • Drop (down) • During (the course of) • Dwindle (down).

Earlier (in time) • Eliminate (altogether) • Emergency (situation) • (Empty) hole • Empty (out) • (Empty) space • Enclosed (herein) • (End) result • Enter (in) • (Entirely) eliminate • Equal (to one another) • Eradicate (completely) • Estimated at (about) • Evolve (over time) • (Exact) same • (Exposed) opening • Extradite (back).

Fall (down) • (Favourable) approval • (Fellow) classmates • (Fellow) colleague • Few (in number) • Filled (to capacity) • (Final) conclusion • (Final) end • (Final) outcome • (Final) ultimatum • (First and) foremost • (First) conceived • First (of all) • Fly (through the air) • Follow (after) • (Foreign) imports • (Former) graduate • (Former) veteran • (Free) gift • (From) whence • (Frozen) ice • (Frozen) tundra • Full (to capacity) • (Full) satisfaction • Fuse (together) • (Future) plans • (Future) recurrence.

Gather (together) • (General) public • GOP (party) • GRE (exam) • Green [or blue or whatever] (in color) • Grow (in size)

Had done (previously) • (Harmful) injuries • (Head) honcho • Heat (up) • HIV (virus) • Hoist (up) • (Hollow) tube • Hurry (up).

Illustrated) drawing • Incredible (to believe) • Indicted (on a charge) • Input (into) • Integrate (together) • Integrate (with each other) • Interdependent (on each other) • Introduced (a new) • Introduced (for the first time) • (ir) regardless • ISBN (number).

Join (together) • (Joint) collaboration.

Kneel (down) • (Knowledgeable) experts.

Lag (behind) • Later (time) • LCD (display) • Lift (up) • (Little) baby • (Live) studio audience • (Live) witness • (Local) residents • Look (ahead) to the future • Look back (in retrospect).

Made (out) of • (Major) breakthrough • (Major) feat • Manually (by hand) • May (possibly) • Meet (together) • Meet (with each other) • (Mental) telepathy • Merge (together) • Might (possibly) • Minestrone (soup) • Mix (together) • Modern (of today) • (Mutual) cooperation • (Mutually) interdependent • Mutual respect (for each other).

(Number-one) leader in • Nape (of her neck) • (Native)

habitat • (Natural) instinct • Never (before) • (New) beginning (New) construction • (New) innovation • (New) invention • (New) recruit • None (at all) • Nostalgia (for the past) • (Now) pending.

Off (of) • (Old) adage • (Old) cliché • (Old) custom • (Old) proverb • (Open) trench • Open (up) • (Oral) conversation • (Originally) created • Output (out of) • (Outside) in the yard • Outside (of) • (Over) exaggerate • Over (with) • (Overused) cliché.

(Pair of) twins • Palm (of the hand) • (Passing) fad • (Past) experience • (Past) history • (Past) memories • (Past) records • Penetrate (into) • Period (of time) • (Personal) friend • (Personal) opinion • Pick (and choose) • PIN (number) • Pizza (pie) • Plan (ahead) • Plan (in advance) • (Please) RSVP • Plunge (down) • (Polar) opposites • (Positive) identification • Postpone (until later) • Pouring (down) rain • (Pre) board (as an airplane) • (Pre) heat • (Pre) record • (Private) industry • (Present) incumbent • Present (time) • Previously listed (above) • Proceed (ahead) • (Proposed) plan • Protest (against) • Pursue (after) • Raise (up).

RAM (memory) • Reason is (because) • Reason (why) • Recur (again) • Re-elect (for another term) • Refer (back) • Reflect (back) • (Regular) routine • Repeat (again) • Reply (back) • Retreat (back) • Revert (back) • Rise (up) • Round (in shape).

(Safe) haven • (Safe) sanctuary • Same (exact) • (Sand) dune • Scrutinize (in detail) • Self- (yourself) • Separated (apart from each other) • (Serious) danger • Share (together) • (Sharp) point • Shiny (in appearance) • Shut (down) • (Single) unit • Skipped (over) • Slow (speed) • Small (size) • (Small) speck • Soft (in texture) [or (to the touch)] • Sole (of the foot) • Spell out (in detail) • Spliced (together) • Start (off) or (out) • (Still) persists • (Still) remains • (Sudden) impulse • (Sum) total • Surrounded (on all sides).

Tall (in height) • Tall (in stature) • (Temper) tantrum • Ten (in number) • Three a.m. (in the morning) • (Three-way) love triangle • Time (period) • (Tiny) bit • (Total) destruction • (True) facts • (Truly) sincere • Tuna (fish) • (Twelve) noon or midnight • (Two equal) halves.

(Ultimate) goal • Undergraduate (student) • (Underground) subway • (Unexpected) emergency • (Unexpected) surprise • (Unintentional) mistake • (Universal) panacea • (Unnamed) anonymous • UPC (code) • (Usual) custom.

(Veiled) ambush • (Very) pregnant • (Very) unique • Visible (to the eye).

(Wall) mural • Warn (in advance) • Weather (conditions) • Weather (situation) • Whether (or not) • (White) snow • Write (down).

13

Biased and Stereotyped Language

Words and phrases that are prejudiced, offensive, and demean are considered to be biased or stereotyped. A writing style that might imply sexual, gender or ethnic bias may be distracting, causing irritation or humiliation, and so should be avoided, out of consideration for the reader. Further, writers are required to "avoid writing in a manner that reinforces questionable attitudes and assumptions about people". To do otherwise is not only offensive, but also can creates bias in both research design and interpretation. Possible areas of bias include the following:

- Gender bias.
- Sexual orientation.
- Ethnicity-related biased and neutral expressions.
- Disability-related bias.
- Age-related bias.
- Miscellaneous biased and neutral expressions.

13.1 Gender Bias

No longer is it acceptable to use masculine pronouns or nouns to refer to persons of both genders who belong to the same group. However, eliminating biased wording may result in twisted, illogical sentences. To eliminate gender bias, consider the following:

Rewrite to change masculine or feminine pronouns to plurals:

- **Incorrect:** The nurse wore her school pin on her collar.
- **Correct:** The nurses wore their school pins on their collars.

Change gender-specific nouns to genderless nouns.

- **Incorrect**: The chairman banged the gavel three times.
- **Correct:** The chairperson banged the gavel three times.
  Avoid invented combinations.
- **Incorrect:** The student may refer to the work as his/her capstone project.
- **Correct:** Students may refer to the works as their capstone projects.
  Avoid alternating gender-specific wording.
- **Incorrect:** The student brought his work to the class and offered her opinions during discussion.
- **Correct:** The students brought their work to the class and offered their opinions during discussion.

Table 13.1 lists some biased words and their neutral alternatives.

Table 13.1: Biased Words and Their Neutral Alternatives.

Biased	Neutral expression
Mankind	Human race
Manmade	Artificial
Manpower	Workforce
Chairman	Chairperson
Salesman	Salesperson/executive
Businessman	Business executive
Foreman	Supervisor
Actor/actress	Actor
Author/authoress	Author
Doctor/lady doctor	Doctor
Housewife	Homemaker
Man hour	Staff hour
Air hostess/steward	Flight attendant
Poet/poetess	Poet
Craftsman	Artisan
Mailman	Mail carrier
Policeman	Police officer
Anchorman	Anchor
Forefathers	Ancestors

Man and wife	Husband and wife
Newsman	Journalist
Middleman	Go-between
Ombudsman	Trouble-shooter
Spokesman	Spokesperson

13.2 Sexual Orientation

The word orientation is generally preferable to *preference*; the terms *lesbians* and *gay* men preferable to *homosexual*. Homosexual is ambiguous and has accrued negative connotations in the past. Again, be specific and precise. In referring inclusively to people whose orientation is not heterosexual, include bisexual people. Be aware of the distinction between sexual behaviour and sexual orientation. In describing behaviour, adjectives are preferable to nouns to clarify this distinction.

For example, same gender, male-male, female-female, male-female sexual behaviour.

- **Incorrect:** The sample consisted of 200 adolescent homosexuals.
- **Correct:** The sample consisted of 200 gay male adolescents. The sample consisted of 100 gay male and 100 lesbian adolescents.

  Comment: Avoid use of homosexual, and specify gender of participants.

13.3 Ethnicity-related Biased and Neutral Expressions

Acceptable phrasing for referring to ethnic groups changes frequently, partly due to personal preferences. Partly, the terms often accrue negative connotations. Again, remember basic guidelines of sensitivity and specificity. Ask about preferred terminology and avoid negatively perceived terms. Black and African-American are currently acceptable. In this context, terms such as Black and White should be capitalised since they refer to ethnic groups and are therefore proper nouns. Avoid biased words (Table 13.2) and use their alternatives.

Table 13.2: Ethnicity-related Biased and Neutral Alternatives

Biased	Neutral expression
Negro/black	African American
Red Indian	Native American
Chinese man	Chinese
Tribal/harijan	Dalit
Oriental	Asian
Mohammedan	Muslim

13.4 Disability-related Bias

Maintain the integrity of individuals as human beings, do not equate the person with the disability, avoid unnecessary negative terms such as victim, (stroke victim) or cripple. Disability refers to an attribute of a person and handicap to constraints on the person, which may include attitudes, physical environment and legislation. Avoid the biased words given in Table 13.3 and use their neutral alternatives.

Table 13.3: Disability-related Biased and Neutral Alternatives

Biased	Neutral expression
Blind	Visually impaired
Deaf	Hearing impaired
Dumb	Speech impaired
Physically handicapped	Differently-abled
Mentally retarded	Intellectually challenged
Lunatic	Insanity/mentally impaired
Defective child	Congenital disability
Fat	Vertically challenged
Tall	Vertically blessed
Bald	Follically challenged
Birth defect	Congenital disability
Spastic	A person with cerebral palsy
Stutterer	A person with speech impediment
AIDS victim	Person with AIDS
Dying of cancer	Living with cancer

13.5 Age-related Bias

Be specific when defining age of participants. Older person is preferable to elderly, which can be considered pejorative and is not acceptable as a noun. Dementia is preferable to senility, although senile dementia of the Alzheimer's type is acceptable.

13.6 Miscellaneous Biased and Neutral Expressions

Some of these are given in Table 13.4.

Table 13.4: Miscellaneous Biased and Neutral Expressions

Biased	Neutral expression
Brotherhood	Kinship
Father land	Native land
Fraternal	Intimate
Mother tongue	Native language
Working women	Wage earner
King size	Jumbo
King maker	Power behind the throne
Lady like	Courteous
Manly	Brave
Maiden name	Birth name
Manpower	Human resources
Man of action	Dynamic
Man of letters	Scholar
Motherly	Loving
St..tesman	Diplomatic
Master peace	Work of a genius
Illegitimate child	Child of un-married persons
Man in street	Ordinary person/lay person
Man-day	Work day
Man handle	Mishandle/damage
Sexual intercourse	Penile-vaginal intercourse

14

The Writing Process

Writing process is important for the following reasons:

1. Having a writing process helps students build confidence in their writing abilities.
2. Having a writing process provides structure and organization to those who might feel lost or unsure of where to start or where to go next with their writing.
3. Having a writing process promotes independence and self-direction amongst young students.
4. Having a writing process supports students in thinking about their writing and not being afraid to revisit and ultimately improve it.
5. Having a writing process supports peer to peer interaction and discourse. Students share their progress with one another and engage in conversations about their work.

In academic writing, we have to learn special conventions. If these conventions are not followed, the meaning may be unclear and the reader may have difficulty in assessing the work. When we write, we do more than just put words together to make sentences. Good writers go through several steps to produce a piece of writing. It is never a one-step action: it is rather an ongoing creative act. When we write, we create ideas, then make a rough draft and polish it by editing and revising. Thus, writing is a process that involves several distinct steps: prewriting, drafting, revising, editing, and publishing. It is important for a writer to work through each of the steps in order to ensure that he has produced a polished, complete piece. The writing process is not always linear. A writer may move back and forth between steps as needed. The process of writing has the following steps:

1. Pre-writing.

2. Drafting.
3. Revising.
4. Editing.

14.1 Pre-writing

It is the first step in writing process. Before we begin to write, we decide what we are going to write about. Then we plan what we are going to write. This process is called pre-writing. It involves the following:

- Choosing a topic and collecting ideas to explain the topic.
- Brainstorming.
- Free writing.
- Outlining.

14.1.1 Choosing a Topic: Sometimes your instructor will give you a list of possible questions or themes, and other times you will have the freedom to choose your own topic. Sometimes the assignment will have a specific purpose (argumentative essay, analysis paper), and other times you will have the freedom to determine the purpose (research paper, term paper). This freedom can be both great and terrifying. If you have trouble choosing what to write about, start with a few ideas and choose the best one after several steps. You can also consult with your instructor about the best topic choice.

A. How to Choose a Topic? Think about things related to the course that you are interested in. If there is nothing which interests you, look through the textbook, instructor-recommended resources, course slides, handouts, and current periodicals for possible ideas.

Narrow a subject by looking at its smaller parts, or by choosing a specific problem, time period, or place to cover. You may need to do a little general research here if you do not know much about the subject. Also asking yourself "Who? What? Where? When? Why? and How?" questions about the subject can help you limit the subject and determine your interests.

Once you have a specific topic for your paper, write your

topic as the question which your paper will answer. Doing this is a great way to focus on your paper and ensure that you meet the paper's purpose. In fact, your purpose will determine the type of question that you ask.

For example, an argumentative paper would probably have a yes/no question, such as "Should the U.S. have used the atomic bomb in World War II?" or "Should the morning after pill be sold to girls under 16?" or "Should animal organs be used for human transplants?" or "Which is a better strategy for the EU to follow to encourage change in Burma—engagement or isolation?" And then, of course, your paper would argue for your answer to the question.

An analytical paper most likely has a why/how question, such as "Why has childhood obesity been increasing in the United States?" or "How has Poland's ban on abortions affected women's lives?" or "How effective is the article in supporting the author's thesis?" or "How could India best reform its agricultural subsidies?" And then, of course, your paper will analyze the various answers, justifying your point of view to the audience. An informative paper often has a what/why/how question, such as "What are the negative aspects of wind energy?" or "What are the causes of anorexia in teenage boys?" or "How can managers evaluate whether to invest money in a software upgrade project?" And then, of course, your paper will explain the various answers, giving the readers a new way of looking at the topic.

B. Things to Remember: You can use certain pre-writing strategies to help you to choose and develop a topic:

- Make a list of ideas on a topic.
- Read and take notes on a topic.
- Make a cluster, which is a visual map of ideas and concepts related to your topic.
- Ask questions about a topic.
- Discuss ideas about a topic with others and take notes.
- Make an outline of your paper.

14.1.2 Brainstorming: Brainstorming is one of the most

important steps in the writing process which one should never skip. When you have a topic, start brainstorming. Write down all the possible answers to your questions, and write down all the information, opinions, and questions you have about your topic. Brainstorming will help you see what you already know, what you think, what you think you know, and what else you need to find out about your topic. Writing things down also ensures that you will not forget your great ideas later.

14.1.3 Free Writing: It simply means getting ideas on paper as fast as one can. Jot down anything that occurs to you, without worrying about order or even making much sense. Write what pops into your mind, without being afraid of making mistakes. Such jottings are not finely reasoned judgments. Many of the ideas are speculative and hastily generalized. Still topics have surfaced and the next task would be to look at them closely, rejecting some, choosing others; and then gathering information.

14.1.4 Outlining: An outline is a way of dividing a subject into its major parts, and dividing these in turn into sub-parts and so on, into finer details. A basic outline is your first attempt to organize the ideas of your paper. It will help you focus your research and consider the order of your ideas. To make one:

A. Choosing and Ordering Points·

1. Write your question and answer (preliminary thesis statement). Don't worry about writing a beautiful, memorable, strong thesis statement yet; just a simple answer to your question is enough to start the basic outline.
2. Write down all the reasons/arguments/effects/solutions (each type of paper is different) you have to answer your question and support your thesis with. Do not look at your sources—use your own brain.
3. Look at your list and organize the ideas. Some may be combined as one larger idea; some may just repeat others in different words. You may decide to delete some too.

4. The remaining ideas will be the main points of your paper. These ideas are the sections of your paper.
5. Decide how to order these points. What order will you follow—chronological, cause to effect, problem to solution, most important to least important, weakest to strongest? Which order will make your paper the strongest and most interesting?
6. Your paper should also cover alternative or opposing viewpoints to show that you have done complete research and considered all ideas. In this "con section," you will present and refute (argue against) other views of your topic.
7. Those are very basic outlines. It is possible to add more to them, especially after a little research. For each section, think of how much support you have. If you have a lot of supporting details (facts, examples, expert opinions) and explanations, then you will need more than one paragraph for that section. Some sections, especially your strongest, need more than one paragraph, while others may have only one.
8. Divide your sections into smaller points. Write the idea of each possible paragraph as a sentence so you can see how/whether it still answers the research question.

To sum up, pre-writing involves exploration of ideas, identifying your audience, compiling resources and giving your writing a logical structure.

14.2 Drafting

This is the second step in the writing process and probably an early version of a piece of writing. As most of us cannot write well at first attempt, we must write and rewrite it. These initial efforts are called drafts which is more spontaneous and active. Once we have planned out our ideas, the next step is to start drafting or writing. During the drafting stage, we should concentrate on getting our ideas on paper, organizing information logically, and developing our topic with enough detail for our audience and purpose. The process of drafting a piece of writing begins with an analysis of the pre-writing. The writer must use his/her pre-writing notes to determine a focus for the piece of writing.

As there are many ways to write the first draft of the paper, the key is to be prepared before we start—have a purpose, a thesis, enough research, and a plan (some sort of outline). And then, just write. We could start at the beginning and write until the end. Or we could write paragraphs separately, in any order we like. Many writers do the body paragraphs first and save the introduction and conclusion for the end.

A draft may have the following form:

- Introduction
- Body
- Conclusion

Things to Remember:

- Drafts are for the writer
- Drafts are not perfect
- Drafts take time

The author begins writing by composing an introduction to the piece. The purpose of the introduction is not only to state the topic of the piece, but it should also draw the reader into the piece of writing. The introduction to a piece of writing should be interesting. Interesting introduction sets the stage for the rest of the rough draft. The tone of the introduction will vary according to the topic. The introduction of an academic paper is usually 1-2 paragraphs long—longer for longer papers with more background information. In general, your introduction should do the following things.

14.2.1 Gain the Immediate Attention of the Audience: Here are some (but not all) of the ways to start an interesting and relevant introduction:

1. Short anecdote that leads to your topic.
2. Surprising statement/fact that relates to your topic.
3. Quotation from a famous person or expert that introduces your topic.

4. Brief and interesting historical review of your topic.
5. Statement which stresses the importance of your topic.
6. Contradiction—someone else's opinion (opposite of yours) about your topic. Use the first sentence (often called the "hook sentence") to hook the readers' interest.
7. Do not be too general! Immediately dive into your specific topic; don't waste space with a general introduction of the entire subject area. Remember that your audience is familiar with the subject area. And never start with the origins of humankind: "Since the beginning of history"!
8. Do not begin with your thesis idea! Use the introduction to build up to your thesis.

14.2.2 Provide any Necessary Background Information or Definition of any Terms:

1. Give only the history, facts, or definitions that readers will need to understand your topic and thesis. Keep in mind what the audience already knows.
2. Use facts/statistics to show the problem if necessary.
3. Avoid dictionary and encyclopaedia definitions if possible and explain in your own words what the important concepts in your paper mean.
4. Use source information to provide background information, but not to answer the research question or give your opinion.
5. Make sure that the readers now know enough to follow your paper, but not too much that they have lost the focus of your paper.

14.2.3 Briefly Introduce the Main Points (Sections) of the Paper:

1. In academic writing, the writers let the readers know what to expect. Provide a brief overview of your paper's main points.
2. Do not support or try to prove these points. Do not go into depth.
3. Do not just write a one-sentence list of your points. You cannot summarize a great idea in one word.

14.2.4 Body Paragraph: Body paragraphs can be written in many ways, depending on your purpose. However, each paragraph should have ONE point which supports the thesis statement. Most body paragraphs will have:

Topic Sentence:

1. Usually, but not always, the first sentence of the paragraph. If it is not the first sentence, it should be very clear which sentence is the topic sentence.
2. It introduces the paragraph's main idea, makes your point about this idea, and relates to the thesis statement.
3. The topic sentence connects to the previous paragraph.
4. The topic sentence is NOT a fact. It has a point of view.
5. The topic sentence is NOT something from a source. It is your idea.
6. Every sentence in the paragraph will support this topic sentence.

Explanation of topic sentence: The sentence(s) after the topic sentence often further describe the main idea of the paragraph.

Support:

1. The topic sentence is supported by supporting points, details, and explanations, often presented in sandwiches. A body paragraph could have one to several sandwiches, depending on how long and in-depth the detail is. Supporting points are the ideas that support the main point of the paragraph. These can be written in your own words and then supported by details.
2. Specific details are very important to show the readers that your ideas are valid.
3. When using facts, examples, studies, experts' opinions, etc. be as specific as possible. Use the experts' names and professions. Use names, places, dates and other specific information about examples. Include numbers and dates. For scientific studies, explain a little about how the study was done. Use vivid descriptions to make the details clear to the readers.

4. Make sure the details are relevant to your point. A common mistake is including misunderstood source information that does not actually support the student's point.
5. Remember that one example does not prove something. Use more than one example or source in a paragraph.
6. Check with your instructor if you can also include your own personal experience as a detail.
7. Clear and complete explanations are very important because the readers are expecting you to explain everything to them. The readers do not expect to have to think too hard. So explain why/how the details support the topic sentence, and thus the thesis.
8. Your explanation should not just repeat the source material, but rather interpret and analyze it.
9. Your explanation should not simply repeat your thesis or topic sentence, but rather explain how the source material supports those ideas.
10. Do not rely on sources too much. It's your paragraph, so it should contain your ideas about the topic as well.
11. Make sure all your support has a logical order and good connection.

Concluding Sentence: The last sentence should review the body paragraph, emphasize the point and/or thesis again, or prepare the reader for the next body paragraph. Do not end the paragraph with a source citation. End with your own idea.

14.2.5 Important Guideline about Body Paragraphs:

1. No long body paragraphs!
2. It is difficult for readers to stay focused on long blocks of text. ¾ of a page is generally as long as a paragraph should be.
3. If your paragraph is much longer, find a logical way to divide it into two body paragraphs.

A writer should complete a rough draft by composing a conclusion. The purpose of a conclusion is to wrap up the piece of writing by connecting all of the related thoughts and ideas. The best conclusions are creative, engaging, and leave few questions unanswered in the mind of the reader. Younger students can conclude a piece of writing with a simple sentence. Advanced writers should include a conclusion paragraph. Conclusion is most important because this is what the reader will remember.

In conclusion, to summarize, at the end are rather boring and typical although they will work. Try to be more sophisticated by repeating or connecting ideas in another way.

Summarize the findings of your paper:

1. Remind the readers of the paper's main ideas and wrap up your argument. Restate the thesis in different words/phrases.
2. Briefly summarize the main points of your paper. Again, say these in a different way, so readers are not bored by repetition of the same sentences and phrases.
3. Use your own thoughts, not your sources. The place for source support was in the body paragraphs, not the conclusion.
4. Do not write any new information, points, or support in the conclusion.

Show the significance of your findings: Explain why your paper is important—What does it mean? What does it solve? What does it say about your topic? What does it show about the future of your topic? What should the readers take away from your paper?

Because academic papers should have a clear organizational structure, throughout your paper, you need to show the readers how your ideas are connected between paragraphs and between sentences. Often this happens naturally as you write; however, sometimes you will need to make the connection clearer to the reader. Here are 3 ways to do this:

Pronouns (he/she/they/this/that/these/those): Use a pronoun to refer to a noun from the previous sentence.

Repeated Words/Ideas: Use the same word or a synonym in the next sentence.

For example: The policy on changing classes is too strict. According to the policy, a student must get the signatures of 7 different people before moving to another class.

Transition Words: These words clearly state the relationship between two sentences. Here are some transitions; if you are not sure what a word means, look it up in a dictionary.

- **To start:** first, first of all, to begin with.
- **To add another idea:** in addition, furthermore, also, moreover, what's more.
- **To add a more important idea:** more importantly, what's worse, what's more.
- **To add your last idea:** finally, most of all, most importantly.
- **To contrast with the previous** idea: however, nevertheless, on the other hand.
- **To show the result of the previous idea:** therefore, thus, consequently, as a result.
- **To emphasize an idea:** in fact, in particular.
- **To give an example of the previous idea:** for instance, for example, to illustrate.
- **To show a time relationship between ideas:** first, second, then, next, finally.

Things to Remember:

1. Set intermediate or small goals. Don't try to do it all in one day. Write daily. Write at the same time of day if that helps.
2. Become familiar with the conventions and jargon that are relevant to your writing project.
3. Read examples of the genre you're working with. Read writing by your editor/advisor. Write an outline or use other kinds of idea generation.
4. Don't expect a perfect piece of writing. A rough draft is supposed to be rough!
5. Write what you can. Save any problems for later. Leave a space or a mark (like an asterisk *).
6. Write a brief note to yourself about what you need to do in

the middle of the text. Write in a natural style. Do not try to sound sophisticated or look for the most formal word.

7. Write the introduction last. Sometimes starting with the methods section can get you started.
8. Students over use transition words. Too many transition words at the beginning of sentences can be annoying. Do not use a lot of transition words. One or two in a paragraph is enough. Students often use them incorrectly.

14.3 Revising

Our first draft is complete, but our paper is far from finished. The next step is to revise our paper which strengthens the content. If drafts are for the writer, revisions are for the reader. During revision, we consider our writing from the readers'/audiences' point of view. In fact, to revise means to re-see or re-look at our writing. While even small changes can make important differences in a written work, revision often means much more than sentence-level editing for grammatical correctness. Importantly, revision is usually the stage of the writing process when the writer takes into account the reader. We can revise individual paragraphs as you finish them as well.

- **Know What to Fix:** Before you can revise, you need to know what to fix. How can you find that out?
- **Get Feedback:** In some courses, you and your classmates will be asked to exchange papers to read and comment on them in class or online. If not, ask a friend to read it. You can also ask your instructor/supervisor to look at parts of your paper (most instructors are happy to help if you have started your paper early. They may not be willing if you ask for advice at the last minute). Listen to the advice of your reviewers, but remember that in the end, your paper is your responsibility.
- **Refer to the Paper Requirements:** Read your paper and look at the requirements or checklist at the same time. Check off what you have, and mark what you need to fix.

- **Outline:** Make an outline of your first draft by listing the main point of each topic sentence. This will show you whether your ideas are clearly organized and whether they focus on answering the research question (the thesis).
- **Read Your Paper for Focus:** Read every sentence of your paper. After each, ask yourself, "Does this support the thesis statement?" If it doesn't, cross it out or change it [Or consider changing your thesis].
- **Read Each Body Paragraph for Support:** Read a body paragraph, and then read its topic sentence again. Did the paragraph support that sentence enough? Were there enough specific details: facts, examples, descriptions, expert opinions?
- **Re-read the Paper as the Audience:** Imagine that you are seeing your paper for the first time (this is often hard to do, which is why it's good to have another person read your paper). As you read, write down any comments or questions your audience might have. Make sure that the tone fits the audience—will the audience be offended or attracted by your writing?
- **Fix it:** Once you know what to fix, you must do it. You will not have a good paper if you are afraid of changing things. It may be easier to completely re-type your paper while just looking at your first draft. How should you change your paper?
- **Erase** words, sentences or paragraphs; eliminate all unnecessary or irrelevant ideas.
- **Add** words, sentences or paragraphs; add new points, details, or explanations.
- **Reorganize** words, sentences or paragraphs; put everything in a logical order.
- **Re-write** words, sentences or paragraphs; keep your ideas but present them better.
- **Revise it Again:** If there is time, revise your second draft. And keep revising. Good writers actually tend to revise more rather than less as they gain more writing experience.

Things to Remember:

1. Check to see if the essay fits the thesis.
2. Make sure each paragraph has a topic sentence.
3. Make sure there are smooth transitions between paragraphs.
4. Check for digressions.
5. Do you have sufficient support in all paragraphs?
6. Is your paper logical in order?
7. Do you have an introduction and a conclusion?

14.4 Editing

While revising focuses mainly on making the content clear for our readers, editing focuses on making our document meet the conventions of standard written English. Upon completion of a rough draft, the writer should take on the first edit of his work. Editing is an ongoing process, not a onetime event. When an author/writer edits his work, he is checking the piece for errors.

Editing should not be a negative process. This is a time to work on creating a polished piece of writing that will make the author proud. Editing will make our writing more precise and easier to understand (not necessarily shorter, but clearer). When editing, we examine every sentence and ask ourselves if it has a purpose and if it is complete, clear, and concise in English. A grammar resource and an English-English dictionary are both helpful editing tools.

14.4.1 Editing Strategies for Specific Problems:

- **Connection between Ideas:** Read the beginning and end of every paragraph to make sure they flow together. Go through the paper sentence by sentence and find connections between them. If the ideas do not connect, add a transition, pronoun, repeated word, synonym, or another sentence.
- **Wordiness:** Find all the very long sentences (25 words or more). Can they be rewritten more clearly and concisely? Read each sentence. After each one, ask, "Is it necessary to

the paragraph? Does it add something new? Could it be eliminated completely or partly? Could it be combined?" Read each sentence word by word. Is every word necessary? Could some be eliminated or re-written in a shorter, clearer way? Could passive verbs be rewritten as active ones?

- **Repetition, Lack of Variety:** Read each sentence and ask, "What is the purpose of this sentence?" Does it introduce a new idea? Does it support or explain the previous idea? Or does it just repeat it? Read the first 5 words of each sentence to find sentences starting in the same way (such as with a transition word). Change some so that your sentences have variety. Look at the length of every sentence. There should be a variety of short and long sentences. Make sentences shorter by dividing them or longer by combining. Find words which are repeated a lot. Use a thesaurus to find other words to use.
- **Sentence Structure:** Go through the essay sentence by sentence. Label the subject(s) and the verb(s) in every sentence. Make sure each sentence has a subject and a verb. Make sure there are not too many subject-verb combinations in each sentence and that word order is subject + verb + object. Fix fragments, run-ons, and word order.
- **Word Choice:** Find all the long words. Could some be replaced with shorter, clearer words? If yes, go for a shorter one.
- **Clarity, Non-English Structure:** Read your paper without using a lot of effort—you are just reading because you are interested in the topic. If you have to read something twice, it is not clear. Read your paper and translate it into your native language in your mind. If it is really easy to translate, then may be the writing is not following the English structure and style. Say your ideas out loud in English. Write exactly what you said. You probably speak more clearly than you write.

14.4.2 Proofreading: When we think our paper is ready to turn it, it is time to proofread (check for mistakes). If we don't proofread, our paper may be full of careless errors, which will show the audience that we were too lazy, rushed, or uncaring to fix our paper. To proofread one should do the following:

1. Do not look at your paper for 24 hours (this requires time management skills)!
2. Print your paper—you will see mistakes that you might not see on a computer screen.
3. Start with the last sentence of your paper and read your paper sentence by sentence, going backwards (This will help you focus on grammar, not content).
4. Cover all the other lines with another piece of paper.
5. Point your pen at each word.
6. Think about the grammar, spelling, punctuation, capitalization, meaning of every word.
7. If you are unsure about anything, use a dictionary or grammar book. If you are still unsure, mark the line and ask someone for help.
8. Fix any mistake that you found.
9. Print your paper and proofread it again!
10. It is a long, slow, unpleasant experience at first. However, the more you proofread, the easier it gets, and the better your English gets.

15

Writing Paragraphs

15.1 What and Why of Paragraphs

A paragraph is a basic structuring unit in a written text. Basically, every paragraph is a building block and should be coherent and consistently represent and flesh out a single idea. Well developed paragraphs are usually a third to half a page in length. The paragraph has the same basic structure as any piece of writing: introduction, main part, and conclusion. It should have what is called *a topic sentence*, near the beginning, which announces the main topic of the paragraph. The paragraph should not deviate much from this topic or introduce any new ones. The first sentence also serves as a transition from the last sentence of the previous paragraph. The final sentence provides a conclusion. It helps to make each paragraph a solid unit that develops a clearly announced sub-topic of the essay.

Structure is an important feature of academic writing. A well-structured text enables the reader to follow the argument and navigate the text. In academic writing, a clear structure and a logical flow are imperative to a cohesive text. Very often longer texts are further divided into sub-sections. These sub-sections are again divided into manageable units; it gives the reader's eyes a rest, and to help the reader understand changes in a longer piece of writing. These small units are called paragraphs. Paragraphs are mini texts, discussing a single idea. To put it in other words, if the text is a journey through our discussion, paragraphs are the stepping stones in that journey which build up the discussion point by point. We start a new paragraph when:

- We express a new or different main idea.
- We explain another part of our subject or step in a process.

- We provide another kind of support for our opinion.
- If the setting time or location of the piece of writing changes.
- When a different person or character speaks.

15.2 Types of Paragraphs

The types of paragraphs we use depend on our purpose of writing. Several paragraphs written about the same subject might be very different, depending on why the writer wrote them. There are four different types of paragraphs:

1. **Narrative Paragraphs** tell us about an event or series of events, usually in a chronological order. Most short stories and newspaper articles are examples of narrative writing.
2. **Descriptive Paragraphs** do exactly what we think they do; they describe a person, an object or a scene in detail.
3. **Expository Paragraphs** are used for explanation. They can list facts, give directions or explain ideas. Writers also use expository paragraphs to define terms, make comparisons and show cause and effect. Since information in expository writing can usually be put into categories, it often uses logical order.
4. **Persuasive Paragraphs** are used to share an opinion about a particular subject. Writers of persuasive paragraphs try to convince readers to agree with the opinions in the paragraphs and sometimes to take action. A persuasive paragraph often uses order of importance.

15.3 Parts of a Paragraph

1. **Topic Sentence:** First sentence in a paragraph introduces the main idea—gives the reader a clear sense of the content—contains words or phrases called controlling ideas. By aptly encapsulating the main idea of the paragraph, the topic sentence indicates to the reader what the paragraph will be about.
2. **Supporting Details:** After the topic sentence—body of a paragraph gives details to develop the main idea of the

paragraph (facts, examples...). The supporting details make up the body of the paragraph. They provide valid points to develop and sustain the main idea of the paragraph. One can include supporting facts, details and examples to strengthen the thrust of the paragraph.

3. **Closing Sentence:** Last sentence of a paragraph—restates the main idea in different words. The closing sentence is the last sentence of the paragraph, and very clearly reiterates the main idea of the paragraph. Try using different words in this sentence rather than repeating the main idea from some sentence already used in the paragraph.

Things to Remember:

- Read the topic very carefully and think about it properly before starting to write.
- Make a rough draft of all the points and thoughts that occur to you while you are brainstorming about the topic.
- Try to include some facts and/or examples pertaining to the topic in this rough draft.
- Narrow down to the main idea of the paragraph.
- Organize the points that you have written down in the rough draft.
- Begin writing by stating the main idea clearly in the first sentence of the paragraph.
- Do not exceed 200 words.
- Read your paragraph carefully after finishing it and check for errors of grammar, spelling, punctuation, etc., and correct them.

15.4 Creating a Perfectly-formed Paragraph:

- Give one main idea—this can be supported and sits in its own paragraph.
- Express your main idea with the topic sentence—a clear statement of the main idea.
- The remainder of the paragraph should give support to the topic sentence.

- Avoid including any more main ideas in this paragraph.
- Start a new paragraph when you find yourself wanting to write a new topic sentence.
- A linking sentence can be put in before the topic sentence if you want to link this paragraph to the previous one.

15.3.1 Avoid the Following When Forming Paragraphs:

- Weak or non-existent topic sentences.
- Short paragraphs with little development of the main idea.
- No development—no supporting evidence or relevant examples.
- Poor transition between paragraphs.
- Placing a single reference at the end of the paragraph when it is obvious that more than one source has been used.

15.5 Paragraph Unity and Coherence

Paragraphs should have both coherence and unity. A paragraph with unity develops a single idea thoroughly and links it to the rest of the paper. Paragraph coherence is achieved when sentences are ordered in a logical manner and when clear transitions link sentences.

15.5.1 Paragraph Unity:

- Develop a paragraph around a major idea. Express this idea in the topic sentence.
- Make the relationship between the main idea of the paragraph and the thesis of the paper clear. Do not assume that the reader will "get it". Spell it out for him/her.
- Support the main idea of the paragraph with details.
- Create separate paragraphs for those details that explore your topic from different perspectives.
- Eliminate sentences that do not support the main idea. Alternately, you may revise the main idea to include those sentences.

15.5.2 Paragraph Coherence: Decide on an order for your sentences that will best develop the paragraph's main idea. Your supporting sentences are raw materials. They will not make sense to a reader unless they are put in order. This order could be based on several factors:

- **Chronological Sequence:** This is useful for describing a sequence of events.
- **Modified Chronology:** Sometimes a major idea presented early in a paragraph can be supplemented with necessary background information.
- **Spatial Position of Different Objects:** This method is useful for description.
- **Conversation between Different Experts:** By moving between a series of key positions, a writer can establish a sense of dialogue and develop a complex argument.
- **Logical Form of Argument:** Some form of logical proof, like a syllogism, can serve as the basis for order.

A. Some Common Connectors:

- **Chronological Connectors:** First,...Second,...Then,... After that,...Finally,...before...after...when...while... during...until,...
- **Facts:** In fact,...That is,...As a matter of fact,...Besides that,...

Examples: For example/For instance,...Furthermore,... Moreover,...Specifically,...

B. Comparison/Contrast Connectors:

- **Comparison Connectors:** Likewise,...Similarly,...In the same way,...also,...too,...the same (as)…
- **Contrast Connectors:** But,...yet,...However,...In contrast,...Although...Even though..., On the one/other hand,...Nevertheless,...Unlike,...Whereas…

C. Cause–Effect Connectors: Therefore,...As a result,...For this reason,...because,...because of,...due to,...since…

16

Extended Writing

16.1 Types of Text

Undergraduate students are often required to develop and express their ideas in extended piece of writing: an essay, a report, or a project/dissertation as a part of their academic activity. The aim of this extended text writing is to provide the students an opportunity to develop their literacy skills, such as:

- Using appropriate sentence forms.
- Writing for purpose.
- To develop appropriate paragraphs.
- Using an appropriate form.
- To develop and express their ideas.
- To provide evidence to support their ideas.
- To display knowledge.

A piece of text may be a single paragraph or a number of paragraphs, each related to the other. The purpose of this writing may be to describe, to explain, to persuade and so on. Depending on the purpose, texts can be categorized as the following types:

- Expository text.
- Descriptive texts.
- Narrative texts.
- Persuasive texts.
- Argumentative texts.

16.1.1 Expository Texts: It explains a concept, an idea, or a situation to others. This act of explaining or making clear with the help of details is known as exposition. When we are trying to explain a concept to the reader, we need to be clear and concise which is the most important thing about expository writing. Examples of expository texts include news articles, information books, and text books. Expository text structures include: cause and effect, concept and definition, proposition and support.

16.1.2 Descriptive Texts: It describes things in order to convey others instructions about a work to be done, physical description of persons, places, objects. While describing any item, it is important to use concrete and specific words for emphasizing its distinctive features. Descriptive texts usually make use of adjectives and adverbs. A good description is a word picture—the readers can imagine the person, place, and object described.

16.1.3 Narrative Texts: Narration is the act of relating a sequence of events. A composition that is in the narrative mode usually deals with an incident, a journey, a visit to a place of interest, or a story. When we narrate something we write about events in the order that they happen and use time order to organize the sentences, as they signal the order in which events happen.

16.1.4 Persuasive Texts: These texts are written to persuade others, to win them over to our point of view. Persuasion depends on how successfully the writer evokes emotions in others. Persuasive writing is found in advertising and newspaper editorials. Persuasive writing requires a good research, awareness of the readers' biases and a solid understanding of both sides of the issue.

16.1.5 Argumentative Texts: In argumentative texts, the writer has to produce a proof or evidence which should convince the reader that the position or belief of the writer is valid. The quality of argument depends largely on the most effective arrangement of evidence. It influences the thoughts or actions of others by using sound reasoning to convince the reader. Hence, we can say, it is a form of rational persuasion writing.

16.2 Text Structure

Text structure refers to the way writers organize

information in a text. Recognizing the underlying structure of content-area texts can help the reader focus attention on key concepts and relationships and anticipate what follows which helps them comprehend as they read. As readers interact with the text to construct meaning, their comprehension is facilitated when they organize their thinking in a manner similar to that used by the writer. Readers who fail to comprehend the text are unable to recognize the organizational structure of that text.

It is obvious that all texts are different to a certain extent, but depending on the writer's purpose, the topic and genre, some texts are organized to employ a few predominant structural patterns. The following structures should be remembered to comprehend the text more effectively:

1. Cause and effect.
2. Sequence.
3. Problem solution.
4. Description.
5. Compare and contrast.

The effective way to determine and identify the text structure is to know the words and phrases that frequently signal organization.

16.2.1 Cause and Effect: In academic writing, events and actions are frequently linked with their cause and effect. A cause and effect text presents how facts, events or concepts result due to other facts, events, or concepts. It is a common method of organizing and discussing ideas in an academic text. It looks at the reason for something, and then discusses the result. Sometimes, the whole text is cause and effect and sometimes it may be only a part. Cause and effects can be organized in either chronological order or in a reverse chronological order. Alternatively, points can be presented in terms of emphasis, from least important to most important, or vice versa. Words that signal this type of text structure are:

- Because of
- Since

- Therefore
- If……then
- As a result of
- Thus
- Hence
- Consequently
- Nevertheless
- For this reason
- Not only—but also
- This led to…..so
- Accordingly
- And so
- Owing to

Signal questions:

- ✓ What happened?
- ✓ Why did it happen?
- ✓ What caused it to happen?

Examples:

The accident occurred **because of…..**

The demand has increased **consequently** the prices are higher.

The prices are higher **as a result of/owing to** an increase in demand.

If you exercise every day, **then** you won't fall ill easily.

Text Example: Natural predators such as snakes, sea gulls, and raccoons are considered threats to the sea turtles, but human beings are considered to pose the greatest threat to the sea turtles. People threaten the turtles if they disturb the nesting sites or harm the sea turtles at sea. Because of these dangers, the Loggerhead sea turtle is considered threatened.

16.2.2 Sequencing: It is sometimes called process writing in which information in a text is organized by order in which it occurs. This method of organizing text is generally used for instructions or directions. We can sequence the information chronologically by taking time and setting in which the information occurred. Generally, information organized sequentially does not occur at any specific time, rather anytime.

It is a form of text in which the writer wishes to inform the reader about certain topics by representing information by listing events in a sequence. Words that signal this type of text structure are:

- First, second……
- Next
- Before
- After that
- Then
- Initially
- Not long after
- At the beginning
- Following which
- Finally
- At the end
- To conclude
- Lastly

Signal questions:

✓ What items, events, or steps are listed?
✓ Do they have to happen in this order?
✓ Do they always happen in this order?

Text Example: During the months from May to September, the Loggerhead turtle comes ashore to nest at night. First the turtle crawls out of the sea to the beach in search of the right place to build a nest for its eggs. Once the location is identified, the turtle digs a hole with its flippers that measures 8" wide and 18" deep. Next, the turtle lays around 120 eggs, the size of ping-pong balls. The turtle then covers the nest by throwing sand over the nest with its flippers. The turtle does this to protect the eggs from predators. Finally, the turtle makes its way back to the sea, and does not return to attend to the nest.

16.2.3 Problem Solution: Writers sometimes organize their text by using problem and solution which may be a real-world or philosophical problem. The writer will present a problem that needs to be solved. This text structure is frequently confused with the cause and effect pattern of organization. The signal words of a problem solution text structure are:

- The question is
- The problem is
- Therefore
- And if.....then
- Propose a solution
- One answer is...
- Problematic
- Remedy
- Prevention
- Fix

Signal Questions:

- ✓ What is the problem?
- ✓ Why is this a problem?
- ✓ Is anything being done to try to solve the problem?
- ✓ What can be done to solve the problem?

Text Example: One problem with the modern Olympics is that it has become very big and expensive to operate. The city or country that hosts the games often loses a lot of money. A stadium, pools, and playing fields must be built for the athletic events and housing is needed for the athletes who come from around the world. And all of these facilities are used for only two weeks! In 1984, Los Angeles solved these problems by charging a fee for companies who wanted to be official sponsors of the games. A company like McDonald's paid a lot of money to be part of the Olympics. Many buildings that were already built in Los Angeles area were also used. The coliseum where the 1932 games were held was used again and many colleges and universities in the area became playing and living areas.

16.2.4 Description: This type of text is used to describe different attributes and features of the subject. It generally begins with an introduction and subsequently the description moves on. The main objective of this type of text is to inform and is widespread in all areas of social life. Description can be done personally (subjective) or impersonally (objective). The main characteristics of a descriptive text are: use of special indicators and adjectives. The signal words of a descriptive text structure are:

- For instance
- For example
- Such as
- To illustrate
- Most important
- In addition
- Further more
- To begin with
- Also

Signal Questions:

- ✓ What specific topic, person, idea, or thing is being described?
- ✓ How is it being described (what does it look like, how does it work, what does it do, etc.)?
- ✓ What is important to remember about it?

Text Example: The Loggerhead is a relatively easy turtle to identify. To begin with, the Loggerhead has a reddish-brown upper shell and a dull brown to yellowish lower shell. The shells consist of an upper part, known as the carapace, and a lower section, called the plastron. Hard scales (or scutes) cover the shells, and the number and arrangement of these scutes are used to determine the species. The adult Loggerhead weighs from 200 to 350 pounds and lives in temperate and sub-tropical waters. Another important fact about this turtle is that it is the most common sea turtle that nests on the shores of the United States. In addition to eating small fish, the Loggerhead sea turtle feasts on shellfish, clams, horseshoe crabs, and mussels. Unfortunately, the Loggerhead turtle is classified as threatened.

16.2.5 Compare and Contrast: Compare and contrast is a

technique that we use every day. It is a text structure where the similarities and differences of two or more things, objects, and ideas are explored. It is a way of establishing relationship between them by comparing and contrasting. When we compare two or more things, we tell what is similar between them. When we contrast things, we tell what is different about them. In literature class, we might have to compare two poems or two characters in a play. The signal words of a compare and contrast text structure are:

- Like
- Unlike
- Both.....and
- Neither
- Similar to
- Different from
- Same as
- As opposed to
- Compared with
- As well as
- Either....or
- Instead of
- Although
- On the other hand
- Unless
- Equal to
- Not only....but also
- In contrast
- Even though
- Where as
- However

Signal Questions:

✓ What things are being compared?
✓ In what ways are they alike?
✓ In what ways are they different?

Examples: Most baby animals can walk within a few hours

of birth. **On the other hand/however/in contrast**, a human baby takes about twelve months to learn this skill (Showing contrast).

Mumbai is the financial capital of India. **Similarly,** Bangalore is the centre for information technology (Compare).

Text Example: The modern Olympics is very unlike the ancient Olympic games. Individual events are different. While there were no swimming races in the ancient games, for example, there were chariot races. There were no female contestants and all athletes competed in the nude. Of course, the ancient and modern Olympics are also alike in many ways. Some events, such as the javelin and discus throws, are the same. Some people say that cheating, professionalism, and nationalism in the modern games are a disgrace to the Olympic tradition. But according to the ancient Greek writers, there were many cases of cheating, nationalism, and professionalism in their Olympics too.

17

Project Writing

An important requirement of many undergraduate courses is that students have to do a piece of research work, referred to as *a project* or *a dissertation*. This work is usually done during the final semester of a three-year degree programme. The project is intended to enable the student to grasp the fundamentals of research, whether theoretical or practical. In other words, a project is a learning vehicle that will enable the student to gain academic and practical skills and, when completed, will demonstrate the students' capabilities. A graduate project thesis represents the culminating experience resulting from a student's graduate study. It is the most important artefact a graduate student creates in earning the degree which shows that a student can perform critical analysis and make a sound technical decision based on the findings.

As a piece of extended academic writing, a project has a definite structure that develops a logical and clear line of thought. A graduate project dissertation is usually divided into chapters and sections that detail the writer's evidence and arguments.

17.1 Aims and Objectives of Project Writing

The aims are the statements by which a student declares their intentions in carrying out the project. They are the purposes that are expected to be fulfilled by doing the project. The general aims depend upon the subject that someone is studying for the degree and the nature of the project that someone chooses to do. The aims and objectives can be summarized in the following ways:

- To test the student's ability to write a formal document.
- To enable the students to design and carry out research in an academic environment.

- To demonstrate the students' ability to formulate a hypothesis and establish a research question.
- To provide opportunity to use research skills acquired whilst on the degree course.
- To encourage the development of an ethical, systematic approach for the selection and use of research methods.
- To encourage the development of an ethical and systematic approach to the collection and use of data or information.
- To test the students' ability to interpret and evaluate data or information gathered during the research.
- To test the students' ability to provide reasoned and objective argument based upon the information obtained by research.

17.1.1 How Big Should the Project Be? An undergraduate project is a small one since it involves only one person—the student. But it appears large for the student as it is a first such piece of work that the student will do and is responsible for its completion. Even though classified as small, undergraduate projects still require careful preparation and planning in order to meet the specified aims and objectives.

17.1.2 Topic Selection: Whatever is the project; selection of the topic for it requires a clear and disciplined preparation as it is not always easy. Some people are fortunate, as the idea for the project may pop into their mind immediately. For many, however, this is not the case, as one may need to be more systematic in search for the project topic that one wishes to explore further. One may have to do a great deal of thinking and background reading before reaching a decision about the topic in which someone wants to invest a lot of time and effort. The following tips may help the students in getting a suitable topic for their project:

- Think about a book you have found interesting.
- Choose a topic that will sustain your interest.
- Choose a topic with some background and existing literature to it.

- Draw upon the unresolved questions and issues that you have studied or intended to study.
- Use reading and knowledge to develop a dissertation question.
- Avoid too broad a topic or one that is overly ambitious.

However, inspirations can come from many sources when looking for a topic. The topic one selects need to be one that can be addressed in an appropriately academic manner within the time constraints of the project work.

17.2 Structure and Contents of Projects

A graduate project/dissertation has different chapters and sections, as it is necessary and invaluable for the students that help to keep track of the flow of the writing and helps the reader/evaluator to make sense of the project without having to strain themselves and fishing for clues. The chapter and section headings should be clear enough to indicate the reader what is in the section. A project dissertation should have the following sections, each of which addresses some basic questions:

1. Abstract of the project.
2. Introduction.
3. Review of literature.
4. Research design.
5. Methodology.
6. Conclusions.
7. Appendix/appendices.
8. References.

17.2.1 Abstract of the Project: The abstract is the hardest part of a project/dissertation to write, and it is the part most readers will read first. So, it should be well-written, clear, and to the point, as it conveys the most important message regarding the project.

Though placed at the beginning and stands independent of the project, the abstract is written when the project is complete in all respects. The abstract includes the thesis statement, the research design, and all the main sections of the project/dissertation in brief.

17.2.2 Introduction: An introduction is the first section of the project dissertation where someone introduces the reader to the particular problem that the project is attempting to solve. It states the project's objectives. If the project has multiple objectives, it is good to state these in a numbered list. The rest of the dissertation describes how someone has accomplished what has been described as the objectives. The introduction also provides a synopsis of what the other chapters contain, in a brief and exact manner. By the time the reader finishes reading the introduction, s/he should have a clear understanding of the problem the project addresses and how it has been solved.

17.2.3 Review of Literature: A literature review for project dissertations is mandatory and is different from the background provided in the introduction. The background provides general information. A literature review focuses on issues that are more specially related to the work in the project. Describe similar works done by others in the past and described in the literature. If any prior work in the literature is not available, then it is most likely that the work is too simple to qualify as a graduate project. The project dissertation needs to demonstrate that the writer has done a literature search and completed a critical analysis of the relevant literature describing prior work in the field. This should be done by writing some discussions on what others have done and the limitations of their work that will show that the writer has done a comprehensive literature search.

A. Locating the Existing Literature: A literature review for project dissertations is conducted by collecting and assessing relevant materials for the current project dissertation. It is always based on secondary sources—that is, what other people have already written on the subject; it is not concerned about discovering new knowledge or information. A literature review will try to look at as much of this existing research as possible. It will not only review major scholarly books in the relevant area, but will also take a keen interest in journal articles, which in many subjects give more up-to-date material.

Preparing a literature review involves the following:

- Searching for reliable, accurate and up-to-date material on the topic or subject.
- Reading and summarizing the key points from this literature.
- Synthesizing these key ideas, theories and concepts into a summary of what is known.
- Discussing and evaluating these ideas, theories and concepts.
- Identifying particular areas of debate or controversy.
- Preparing the ground for the application of these ideas to new research.

Make sure that all the literature you review is as up-to-date as possible. The sole exception would be 'classic texts' such as major works written by the leading scholars setting out formative ideas and theories central to your subject.

B. Writing up the Literature Review: As with any other pieces of academic writing, only attempt to write up the literature review when it is 'ripe'—that is, when you have done all the reading, note-taking and planning for the chapter or section. Your literature review should have an introduction, a main body, and a conclusion. The introduction establishes the context of your research, outlines any issues which have inspired your research interest, and indicates why your research is important. Clarify the scope of your review, so that the reader knows what you will and won't be addressing.

The body or your review summarizes and synthesizes your material. Keep the focus of your review at the forefront of your mind when writing, so you only include relevant material which evidences your arguments and observations. Remember to relate it to your own research.

The conclusion should summarize your critique of the literature and identify any gaps or issues arising from the existing research. Conclude by explaining how your research attempts to address these gaps or build on the existing research. Write in a formal, academic style, using language which is clear, concise, and objective.

17.2.4 Research Design: Research design is the overall plan for connecting the conceptual research problems to the pertinent (and achievable) empirical research. It is the structure of any research. Research design articulates what data is required, what methods are going to be used to collect and analyze this data, and how all of this is going to answer your research question. There are different types of research designs which have both advantages and disadvantages. The frequently used research designs are:

- Descriptive studies.
- Content analysis.
- Discourse analysis.
- Historical method.
- Scientific method.
- Experimental method.

17.2.5 Methodology: The methodology section of the project dissertation answers two main questions: how was the data collected or gathered? And, how was it analysed? Methodology is important for any branch of scholarship because an unreliable method produces unreliable results and, as a consequence, undermines the value of researcher's interpretation of the findings.

A. Meaning of Data: Data can be defined as a collection of facts, figures or any other related material, which has the ability to serve as the information for the basic study and analysis. It must be kept in mind that data related to the questions or the queries are very much needed. Data acts as the back bone for the analysis, so it can be said that no guess work or opinions can ever make a place in the research since the other factors play a critical role in the research. Data can be either old in nature or it may be the current one.

B. Types/Sources of Data: Depending on the discipline, data types and sources can be represented in a variety of ways. The two primary data types are quantitative (represented as numerical figures, interval and ratio level measurements), and qualitative (text, images, audio/video, etc.). Although scientific disciplines differ in their preference for one type over another, some investigators utilize information from both quantitative and qualitative sources with the expectation of developing a richer understanding of a targeted phenomenon. Data sources can include books, field notes, journals and periodicals, interviews, laboratory notes/specimens, or direct observations of humans, animals, plants.

There are three types of sources used for writing research papers: primary, secondary, and tertiary. Knowing how to distinguish among them is an indispensable skill in academic writing.

- **Primary Sources:** Primary sources offer first hand information about the subject under discussion which is the original source of information. Examples of primary sources include books, novels, films, visual art, musical scores, diaries, letters, artefacts, legal documents, eyewitness accounts, and original research and so on. In natural and social sciences, primary sources are often empirical studies which are found in scholarly journals or conference papers that report on research undertaken by their authors.
- **Secondary Sources:** Secondary sources provide analyses of primary sources. They provide information about original information which help you understand and evaluate primary source material. Use secondary sources to situate your research within a larger context, keep up with current theory, find models for your research, and discover other viewpoints and alternative theories. Most importantly, use secondary sources to support your interpretation of primary texts or to refute those who disagree with your opinion. Secondary sources include book reviews, commentaries, scholarly books and articles written for research purposes as well as specialized

reference works.

- **Tertiary Sources:** Tertiary sources furnish information compiled from summaries of or commentaries on primary and secondary sources. Use tertiary sources to gain a general overview and better understanding of your topic and to weed through large amounts of information quickly and efficiently. Consult them for research purposes only and not for evidence to support your analysis. Tertiary sources include textbooks, abstracts, manuals, and indexes. Dictionaries and encyclopaedias are also considered tertiary sources unless they provide scholarly analysis.

A combination of all these three sources is used in the literature review to answer the research questions, depending on the type of source it requires.

C. Methodology for Data Analysis: There are a variety of methods that one can choose to investigate a research problem. The methodology section should clearly articulate the reasons why someone should choose a particular procedure or technique. Choice of the method should be appropriate to fulfilling the overall aims and objectives of the study and should be consistent with the accepted practice in the field of study.

Data can be collected and analyzed by using the following methods:

- Qualitative methods.
- Quantitative methods.
- Quasi methods.

The quantitative approach involves collection and analysis of numerical data and applying statistical tests, while quantitative approach is more subjective in nature and involves examining and reflecting on perceptions in order to gain an understanding of social and human activities. Quantitative methods are usually regarded as more robust, leading to actionable results and recommendations. The quantitative data analysis gives a research more direction and is viable for readers by numeric interpretation of responses to the questionnaires given out. Using quantitative method of analysing is rational. The quantitative data analysis has been used in the research by quantifying responses from the management, staff and students of the organisation via questionnaires.

Qualitative approach is the nature and content of what is said while quantitative approach determines the number of who said it. Van Maanen (1983) defines qualitative techniques as an array of interpretative techniques which seek to describe, decode, translate and otherwise come to terms with the meaning, not the frequency, of certain more or less naturally occurring phenomena in the social world. Qualitative research is thus common in social and behavioural sciences and among practitioners who want to understand human behaviour and functions. Since this research has to do with social sciences, it makes qualitative analysis relevant to the research.

Quantitative approach to data collection provides relative ease and speed with which research can be conducted. Qualitative method of data analysis can be described as the interactive way where collected data are analyzed initiating new questions and further data collection.

Quasi methods use combinations of both quantitative and qualitative methods required by a particular research design. One has the freedom of choosing any one of these methods depending on his/her research design.

17.2.6 Conclusions: The conclusion chapter summarizes the problem you set out to solve; describe what you have achieved, and the prospect for future work. The conclusion should not contain detailed description of the problems or the solutions.

17.2.7 Referencing: Academic writing, particularly when it is formally assessed, has to follow certain rules and conventions. Among the most important of these are the rules and conventions about citing and referencing the work of others. These help distinguish academic material from other forms of writing. When you are writing a piece of work and use someone else's words or ideas you must reference them. This means that you need to include detailed information on all sources consulted, both within your text (in-text citations) and at the end of your work (reference list).

A citation or reference is a way of properly acknowledging the use of work of others. "Citing" means giving such an acknowledgement within the main body of a piece of work, while "referencing" is a broader term which covers both in-text citations and the more extensive information about your source material which should be presented at the end of your work. Apart from allowing your readers to consult your references, this also gives authority to your work by demonstrating the breadth of your research.

Referencing is crucial to successful research because of the following reasons:

- Helps the reader to find the original source if they wish.
- Improves your writing skills.
- Adds authenticity to your argument.
- Shows that you have read widely.
- Can help you get better marks.

Sources of referencing may include (but are not limited to):

- Published works such as journal articles or books (including any textbooks set by the course or module—even if markers know exactly where something comes from, you must still state it clearly).
- Grey literature such as conference proceedings or reports from organizations and government agencies.
- Material from the internet, whether or not it has a named author.
- Unpublished material such as lecture/tutorial notes or other students' work.
- And even exchanges such as emails or conversations with other people (be it staff, students, friends or others).

If you wish to make use of any of your own previous work, e.g. elements of essays you previously did for other assessments, you should indicate and cite this as clearly as any other source.

There are many well-recognized citation formats to meet the conventions of the field you are working in. One can follow the MLA (Modern Language Association), the APA (American Psychological Association) or any other accepted standard format: Chicago Manual of Style, AMS (American Mathematical Society), CSE (Council of Science Editors) and AMA (American Management Association) in all citations and references. It is normally up to you to decide which system you would like to use. MLA style is most commonly used to write papers and cite sources within the liberal arts and humanities.

It is a research and publications association of research scholars that prepares the standard formatting of research writing and citations accepted by all the universities.

When we quote, refer to a source or paraphrase, we have to provide the source in the text that will allow the readers to locate the full citation in the works cited section. In this type of citation, we use the second name of the author and page number without any punctuation.

Example: Wordsworth stated that romantic poetry was marked by a "spontaneous overflow of powerful feelings" (263).

The above example tells readers that the information in the sentence can be located on page 263 of a work by an author named Wordsworth. If the readers want more information about this source, they can turn to the works cited page, where, under the name of Wordsworth, they would find the following information:

Wordsworth, William. *Lyrical Ballads*. OUP, 1967.

If we use a source by two authors, we have to list the authors' last names in the text.

Example: The authors claim that surface reading looks at what is "evident, perceptible, and apprehensible in texts" (Best and Marcus, 9).

Things to Remember:

- The in-text citation usually appears in parentheses and

corresponds directly to an entry in your list of works cited.

- The author's last name and the page number are usually enough to indicate the location in the source.
- If the author's name is used in the sentence, do not repeat it in the citation.

17.2.8 Appendix/Appendices: An appendix (one item) or appendices (more than one item) is information that is not essential to explain your findings in the project dissertation. However, this information may support your analysis and validate your conclusions. Some of these items may have been written by you or printed/photocopied from elsewhere. Use appendices to present material that will interrupt the flow if included in the main body of the project dissertation. The contents of appendices include:

- Supporting evidence (e.g. raw data that is referred to in the text).
- Contributory facts, specialised data (raw data appears in the appendix, but summarised data appears in the body of the text).
- Sample calculations (referred to in the text).
- Technical figures, graphs, tables, statistics (referred to in the text).
- Detailed description of research instruments (referred to in the text).
- Maps, charts, photographs, drawings (referred to in the text).
- Letters, copies of emails (referred to in the text).
- Questionnaires/surveys (questionnaire/survey results appear in the body of the text).
- Transcripts of interviews (summarised in the text).
- Specification or data sheets (summarised in the text).

A. Format and Positioning of Appendices:

- Appendices may follow the reference list.
- Each appendix must begin on a new page.
- The order they are presented in is dictated by the order they are mentioned in the text of the report.

- The heading should be written as APPENDIX (upper case) or Appendix (sentence case), followed by a letter or a number. Centre the title of each appendix, and change to bold type e.g. APPENDIX A, Appendix 1. Be consistent in your choice of style.
- Appendices must be listed in the table of contents (if used).
- The page number(s) of the appendix/appendices will continue on with the numbering from the last page of the text.

17.3 Project Writing Style

- Write short sentences in active voice in plain language. Each sentence should address a single topic.
- Paragraphs should be short, focused, and coherent. Each paragraph should have a clearly stated topic sentence that describes the main issues covered in the paragraph.
- Provide heading for all the chapters and sections.
- Number all figures and tables used in the project dissertation.
- Figures, tables, and their associated captions should be centrally justified.
- Do a grammar and style check.

17.4 Sample Format of a Project Dissertation

Cover page
Table of contents
Title page
Certificate page
Acknowledgement page
Abstract
Chapter One: Introduction
Chapter Two: Literature review
Chapter Three: Research Design
Chapter Four: Research methodology
Chapter Five: Discussion

Chapter Six: Conclusion
Works Cited
Bibliography (optional)
Appendix

18

More on Academic Writing

18.1 Writing a Term Paper

A *term paper* is originally a written assignment (usually a research based paper) that is due at the end of the *term*—either a semester or a quarter. It is based on an independent research into one of the themes either suggested by the student or by the supervisor. In a term paper, a student should demonstrate his/her ability of finding the relevant sources, selecting, eliciting and logically organizing the information on the topic, data gathering, processing, summarizing and analyzing the same. However, not all term papers involve academic research, and not all research papers are term papers.

The topic of a term paper might be chosen by the student or sometimes it might be a prompt given by the professor of the subject. In the latter case, the professor provides you a problem to resolve or a question to examine and sets the requirements for the paper. However, sometimes the professor might not give you very much information but just a very general task.

A term paper can be a critical essay on a popular or current topic requiring author's personal point of view of the issue and demonstration of good and accurate understanding of the subject. The author needs to establish compelling arguments accompanied by facts or other evidence supporting his/her point of view.

A term paper can also be a research paper on a topic chosen by the student and involving thus more thorough academic research in the chosen subject. However, it is very probable that you need to select a topic or subject that had been discussed in the class or in a relevant text book. In this case, the requirements are basically the same as of a research paper, starting with choosing a feasible topic which interests and/or challenges you and that has a sufficient range of references available.

The required amount of words is 9,000-12,000 (30-40 pages) without appendices. The number of bibliography sources used for devising a term paper is about 8-10.

18.1.1 Why is it Important? Since a term paper is a kind of practice in academic writing, it is useful and important for the following reasons:

- A term paper is an opportunity to show that you are capable of researching and arguing about a subject independently.
- It teaches you to give information and express ideas in a clear, systematic way.
- It provides a much deeper knowledge of that area which can be helpful for others in their research.

18.1.2 Components of a Term Paper:

A. Preliminaries:

(a) Title Page: A title page contains the following:

- The title of your paper,
- Your name and student number,
- The course name and code,
- The instructor's name, and
- The due date.

(b) Abstract: An abstract is a brief summary of the main ideas of your term paper usually in about 100 to 200 words. The main elements are as follows:

- A short statement of your research nature or subject ,
- A brief description of your general theoretical approach and research methods, and
- A short summary of your main arguments and research findings.

(c) Table of Contents: A table of contents provides an analytical outline of your paper with the sequence of your presentation. A table of contents should list out:

- The heading of every division of the paper.

- The subheadings of every sub-section within the divisions (if any).
- Page number for every division and subsection.

B. Text:

(a) Introduction: An introduction should be an interesting opening to show the main theme and specific topics of your paper. An introduction usually forms through:

- A concise and complete statement of your research question or the general purpose of your term paper.
- A justification for your study (the significance).
- A background to your research question and a review of the relevant literatures on it (literature review).
- A brief statement of the sources of data, the procedure or methods of analysis (methodology).
- A preview of the organization of the paper.

(b) Main Body (Chapters or Sections): Since the topics of term papers are so diverse, it is impossible to give specific indications of how to write the main body of a term paper. But, the general rule is that you must organize your presentation in a logical framework with a clear conceptual linkage among sections and give every point, a substantial support from the concrete source.

(c) Conclusion: A conclusion should provide a firm ending of what you have discussed in the paper and, preferably, further to reach a judgment, to endorse one side of an issue, or to offer directives. A good conclusion usually contains:

- A recapitulation of the main findings or main themes.
- Statements about the specific values or alternative insights of your paper for understanding the subject matter.
- Indications of the important relevance to the current circumstance or future possibility.
- Suggestions for policy as per your findings.

C. Reference Materials: At the end of your paper, you must provide a reference list in an alphabetical order by the surname of the author. If you use the title bibliography, you can list out both references cited in the text and the relevant works which have consulted. If you use the title references, you should only list out the references cited in the text.

As already discussed, different institutions have developed different styles of documentation. No matter which one you use for your paper, the principle is to be consistent. A term paper must have a clear documentation of all reference materials used in the text. This requires that your paper must indicate from where you obtained:

- Direct quotations.
- Borrowed ideas (including paraphrases and summaries).
- Data and cases (if they did not come through your own research).

You should include the following information about each source:

- Author's name,
- Title of the book ,
- Name of the editor, translator, or compiler,
- Edition used,
- Numbers of the volumes used,
- Name of series ,
- Place of publication, name of the publisher, and date of publication, and
- Page numbers (if it is an essay or a chapter).

The author's name appears first. The title of the book appears in italics. Subtitles follow after a colon. The year of original publication (for all primary texts and for secondary texts that were initially published more than thirty years ago) and the edition follow the title. Place of publication is followed by a colon, and then the publisher and date of publication are separated by a comma. If the book is part of a series, this piece of information should appear after the title of the book.

An article from a scholarly journal appears within double quotation marks. The name of the periodical is italicized and immediately followed by the volume number. The date of publication is written in parentheses followed by a colon and the page numbers.

Chapters in books or contributions in scholarly volumes also appear in double quotation marks (as do short stories and poems); in everything else they follow the format for books.

Always italicize the titles of works published independently (monographs, volumes, periodicals, etc.). Place other titles (articles, chapters, etc.) in quotation marks. Do not forget to format titles correctly even when they are a part of another title. If an entry in the works cited/bibliography runs longer than one line, indent all subsequent lines.

18.2 Writing a Research Proposal or Synopsis

18.2.1 What is a Research Proposal? A suitable research proposal is a pre-requisite for acceptance into a master's or doctoral programme. This document informs the respective faculty as regards the potential candidate's ability to complete the proposed research. In this regard, the primary purpose of the research proposal is to provide information about the intended research project, in terms of content and methodology, in order to assess both the feasibility of the project and the intended modus operandi to be undertaken by the candidate in the months ahead. Thus, a research proposal is an outline of your proposed research project that is designed to:

- Define a clear question and approach to answering it.
- Highlight its originality (doctoral level only) and/or significance.
- Explain how it adds to, develops (or challenges) the existing literature in the field.
- Persuade the potential supervisors of the importance of the work, and why you are the right person to undertake it.

Research proposals may vary in length, but generally speaking, a proposal should be no more than 2,500 words, or 5 pages in length; 2-3 pages are normally sufficient.

18.2.2 What is the Research Proposal For? Potential supervisors use research proposals to assess the quality and originality of your ideas, your skills in critical thinking and the feasibility of the research project. Research proposals are also used to assess your expertise in the area in which you want to conduct research, your knowledge of the existing literature (and how your project will enhance it).

18.2.3 Structuring the Research Proposal: The candidate's research proposal will be assessed in terms of both its content and form. It should be professionally presented, typed and written in grammatically correct English. The proposal must be well structured and logical, with clearly indicated section headings. The following elements are crucial in a good research proposal:

A. Title: You must provide a working title for your research, this is likely to change over time, but provides a good starting point for your proposal.

B. Introduction: You should introduce the questions and issues central to your research and explain how your research will benefit the field.

C. Research Background: Expand on the information you have given in your introduction and try to answer the following questions:

- What are the key texts already existing in your field?
- How does your proposal differ from the existing research?
- What will your project contribute to existing works in the field?
- How does your project expand our understanding and knowledge of the subject?

You must set out your research questions as clearly as possible and explain the problems you want to explore.

D. Research Methods: Show how you plan to carry out your research:

- Does your project involve archives, databases or specialist libraries?
- Is your study interdisciplinary?
- What are the theoretical resources you intend to use and why?
- Is your research based on a single author or a group of

writers and texts?

E. Theoretical Framework: This section will detail the theory that is guiding the proposed study and the logic of using the approach/es.

F. Research Design: Discuss the proposed research design of the study, whether it is a survey, experiment, observation and explain how the design will derive results. The process of data collection and the sources is to be mentioned.

G. Analysis and Discussion: This section states how analyzing the data in the proposed manner would answer the research question and their importance.

H. Timetable: Set out your timescale for completing your study. You need to think about dividing your research into sections and indicate how you plan to write up each section.

I. Reference: This section includes all references, which lists the books and articles, you have referred to in the proposal.

18.2.4 What Makes a Strong Research Proposal? A strong research proposal has the following features:

- Formulates a precise, interesting research question.
- Establishes the relevance and value of the proposed research question in the context of current academic thinking.
- Describes and evaluates the data or source material your research requires.
- Outlines a clear and practical methodology, which enables you to answer the research question.
- States clearly what you hope to discover at the end of your research and what new areas it might open up.

18.2.5 Proofread Your Research Proposal: It is essential that you use accurate information and correct punctuation and spelling in your research proposal. Write in clear sentences and ensure that your research proposal is structured in a logical and easy to understand format. Ask someone else to proofread your research proposal and check it for any errors before submitting it.

18.3 Writing a Research Paper

Writing a research paper is like the task of a sculptor. The investigator chips away extraneous data from the gathered information and begins to sculpt his large block of research into an artistic creation. Anyone can learn to write a good research paper. Unlike creative writing, a research paper is based on a standard format, expectations, and stylistic guidelines that anyone can follow.

A research paper, also called an article, is an academic work that contains original research results and offers a unique perspective or answer after investigating a topic by accumulating primary and secondary sources. It is very different from a report of a topic by summarizing the primary and the secondary sources.

The results and findings of an investigation can be presented through two major research writing forms: argumentative and analytical.

- **Argumentative Paper:** An argumentative research paper persuades the readers to accept a theory or point of view that is debatable. The researcher offers a stance in the introduction and in the thesis statement and then argues in favour of his/her position. Using the sources, the researcher convinces the readers of his/her viewpoints.
- **Analytical Paper:** An analytical paper is to explore the answer to a question about a topic. Writers do not stick to a particular side. They analyse a range of viewpoints and include enough support based on a strong scurce. This way, readers can make their own conclusion.

18.3.1 Finding a Topic: Perhaps the most difficult part of any research paper is finding an adequate topic, formulating a title and making a coherent argument. Once you have decided on a topic or a title, which in literary studies will most likely involve a certain text, rephrase it as a question to guide your research. You should also think about the methodology you intend to apply to your analysis.

If you have access to an annotated edition of your chosen

text, make good use of the materials this offers you. Read both the text itself and the additional material carefully whilst taking notes. This will be the basis for your subsequent research.

Try to summarize and organize your findings systematically. Figure out which aspects belong together, find contradictions and the correspondences. A good place to start is with your own questions—don't be afraid of the questions you have about the text, more likely than not, they are the ideal starting point for your study.

18.3.2 Write a Thesis Statement: Once you have settled on a topic and perhaps even come up with a title, you need to develop a thesis statement. A thesis statement is a succinct formulation of your topic in terms of argument, i.e. your thesis statement must be arguable, and you are stating an opinion that will be proven in the course of your paper with the help of sources. A good way to come up with a thesis is to generate questions surrounding your chosen topic. For example, "In Shakespeare's tragedy work, Romeo and Juliet, love is less an emotional state than a framework for the construction of a social struggle".

18.3.3 Draft an Introduction: Although writing an introduction may seem intimidating this early on, it will force you to focus your research process and prevent unnecessary diversions. Try to explain your topic, legitimate its importance and introduce the approach you intend to take. Regard this as the rough draft of an introduction; a working product.

18.3.4 Write an Outline: What you are trying to do when writing an outline is to come up with a systematic classification of the elements of your argument. You need to develop categories and relationships between and within these categories that will give your paper a structure. Ideally, your outline will be derived from your topic and will help guide your research. It is also a preliminary table of contents. Outlines can be structured in a temporal order (beginning, climax, end), a logical order (a fact and its causes and consequences), or a rhetorical order (from the general to the specific, from the specific to the general from the simple to the complex, etc.). Which structure is best will depend on your specific paper.

18.3.5 Writing Your Paper:

Collect and organize your notes systematically. There is no all-for-one-solution available when it comes to organizing your thoughts, so take the time and experiment with different systems until you find or develop one that works best for you. You might try the following:

- Write one thought per note card in a full sentence. Write the source in the upper right hand corner to keep track of your citations. Be very precise in noting whether you are taking down a direct quote or whether you are paraphrasing an idea. Whenever possible, paraphrase ideas and save direct quotations for remarks that are absolutely essential.
- If you have a laptop, you can save a lot of time by typing your citations into the computer and organizing them virtually. This way you don't have to type up your handwritten note cards. And of course, typed text is always flexible and can be moved around according to your needs.
- Depending on the scope of your paper, you may want to consider keeping a notebook where you can jot down your ideas. If you get a small one then you can carry it around and keep track of your ideas even when you are on the train, plane or in a bus etc.
- There are three main types of taking notes: *summarizing, paraphrasing,* and *quoting*. Always think about the appropriate method for the task in hand. Be sure to be precise in your note taking and to document your sources accurately! Do not take too many notes. There comes a time when you will have to start writing!

General aspects to consider:

- Don't be afraid to discard!
- Write at least two drafts!
- Beware of plagiarism!

A. Contents:

- Avoid lengthy biographical tangents and plot summaries.
- If your argument does require a plot summary, write it in the present tense.
- Your argument should be supported by quotations (cf. below).
- Your introduction should not only describe your topic and its importance, it can include a thesis statement and indicate the method you will be applying. You may also include a brief analysis of the main sources relevant to your topic.

B. Style:

- Observe the general conventions for expository writing.
- Present your ideas precisely and effectively in the formal style appropriate for a research paper.
- Observe coherence and readability of your presentation.

C. Form:

- **Conventions:** Type your paper; format: DIN A4 paper, font: Times New Roman/Arial/Courier/Calibri, font size: 12 pt, line spacing: double, sufficient margins (left: 4 cm, right: 2 cm).
- **Pagination:** Includes the cover page which is not given a page number.
- **Title Page**: Indicates the title of the research paper, the name of the author, the title of the seminar and the name of the lecturer, and the date of submission.
- **Table of Contents:** Gives headlines which will reappear throughout your paper and give it structure. Your table of contents will usually develop out of your outline and should reflect the organizational principles you have chosen for it. Avoid too many subdivisions which may distort the overall coherence of your argument.

D. Works Cited/Bibliography:

- The works cited list at the end of the research paper gives a detailed synopsis of all primary and secondary sources you have consulted. Note that the works cited section should give a complete list of the works referred to in the text, including readings in the field which do not appear in quotations and footnotes.

- Alphabetize entries in the list of works cited by the author's last name, using the letter-by-letter system. Alphabetical listing helps your reader to find full publication information of works referred to in the text. In cases of anonymous authorship, list the first noun of the title.
- Differentiate between a works cited list and a bibliography. Whereas the former references only those sources referred to in your paper, the latter gives additional relevant sources.

E. Sections of a Research Paper:

- Title of the paper,
- Abstract,
- Key terms,
- Introduction,
- Methodology,
- Discussion,
- Conclusion
- Reference, and
- Appendix (if required).

F. Why Key Terms? Key words typically allow readers to judge whether or not an article contains material relevant to their interests, and provide readers with suitable terms to use in web-based searches to locate other materials on the same or relevant topics.

18.4 Writing Book Reviews

Book reviews play an important part in academic writing and is a special kind of academic writing. A book review is an opportunity to evaluate the strengths and weaknesses of a book. It is a form of literary criticism in which a book is analyzed based on content, style, and merit. It follows a well-known structure and components. The objective of a book review is to evaluate how well the authors have achieved their purpose. The review should describe the purpose and explain how they have tried to achieve it. The reviewer should state how well he believes the authors have achieved their purpose, supporting his conclusions with evidence from the book. A book review may raise both positive and negative points supported by evidence from the book.

18.4.1 Language of a Review: The tone of the review should reflect a courteous and gracious attitude. Even if one disagrees with the author, write in a collegial manner and do not use combative language to humiliate those who hold opposite views.

18.4.2 Background:

- The story is set…
- The story takes place …
- This well-written/informative/fascinating book…
- This original first novel…
- The book tells the story of…
- The book/novel was written by…
- This work is based on…

Main points of the plot:

- The book relates how...
- The plot focuses on...
- The story begins/concerns/is about…
- The plot has an unexpected twist…
- The plot is (absolutely) thrilling...

18.4.3 General Comments and Opinion:

- It is rather confusing/long/slow/boring.
- It has a tragic/surprising/dramatic end.
- It is beautifully/poorly/badly written.
- The story is gripping.
- It is an inspiring story.
- It's a fast-paced story.
- This book is brilliantly plotted.
- This book is a non-stop reading.

18.4.4 Useful Language: Recommendations

- Do not miss it.
- It is well worth reading.
- It will change the way you see.
- I wouldn't recommend it because...
- I highly/thoroughly recommend it.
- It is a highly entertaining read.
- It is a bore to read.
- It is certainly at the top of my list.
- It is a must.
- Do not bother with this one.

18.4.5 Length of a Book Review: The preferred length for book reviews is about 1,000 words. This may be extended slightly for a particularly important book, or reduced for one which does not need extended treatment.

18.4.6 Steps of a Book Review: The first step in doing a book review is to read the book carefully and take notes. One should read it at least twice, preferably with a gap between the two readings. In the first reading, familiarise yourself with the book and form initial impressions. In the second reading, test your impressions and gather evidence to support your conclusions.

Some questions to keep in mind while reading a book:

1. What is the book's argument?
2. Does the book do what it says it is going to do?
3. Is the book a contribution to a field or a discipline?
4. Does the book relate to a current debate or trend in the field and if so, how?
5. What is the theoretical lineage or school of thought out of which the book rises?
6. Is the book well-written?
7. What are the book's terms and how are they defined?
8. How accurate is the information (e.g., the footnotes, bibliography, dates etc.)?
9. Are the illustrations helpful? If there are no illustrations, should there have been one?

10. Who would benefit from reading this book?
11. How does the book compare to other books in the field?
12. If it is a textbook, what courses can it be used in and how clear is the book's structure and examples?

Book reviews contain the following key features:

1. Accurate details of the authors'/editors' names and initials.
2. Title of the publication.
3. Edition.
4. Date of publication.
5. Publisher and place of publication.
6. ISBN number.
7. Format (hardback, paperback or soft cover).
8. Number of pages.
9. Price.
10. An early paragraph saying what the book is about, and putting it in the context.
11. Information about the intended audience.
12. A critique of the argument/content of the book.
13. Any supporting academic references.
14. Remarks on the strengths and limitations of the book.
15. A note on the format, length and price (or value for money).
16. A note (if appropriate) on how well the text is supported by tables/diagrams/illustrations.
17. One might structure the review by using the following four components as headings:

- Details of the book.
- Background of the author.
- Description of the purpose.
- Evaluation of the book.

Or one may write it in an essay format. If one writes the review in an essay format, it should be arranged around the central thesis of the evaluation and should use the normal three-part structure: introduction, body and conclusion.

18.4.7 Things to Remember:

- Provide a page number for every quotation, e.g. (p. 17). In the case of edited volumes with multiple authors, please also mention the author of any quotations, e.g. (Hashmi 5).

- Use double quotation marks around shorter quotes of 40 words or less. Set larger quotations off from the text in a freestanding block with no quotation marks.
- Do not use too many quotes from the book. It is best to paraphrase or use short telling quotes within the sentences.
- Keep references to a minimum and present them at the bottom of the review.
- Double-space throughout, including citations, and provide one-inch margins.
- Do not include footnotes or tables.
- At the end of the review, to the right of the page, include your name, institution and location.
- Do not cover everything in the book.
- Judge the book by its intentions, not yours.

18.5 Writing Reports

18.5.1 What is a Report? A report is a highly structured document written in a formal style. Normally, a report is based on your reading and some form of practical work, such as an investigation, survey, experiment or review of practice in other organizations.

Reports are written for a particular purpose, to inform, to persuade, or to offer recommendations. They are also produced for a specific audience. Reports generally draw conclusions based on their findings and may suggest a course of action or areas of further research.

Reports generally aim to:

- Set out the issue and explain why the activity was undertaken.
- Describe what was done and how it was done.
- Present the findings, conclusions, and recommendations.

18.5.2 Preparing and Writing Your Report: Use your assignment brief to make sure you understand the purpose of the report and the intended audience. Have a plan allowing enough time to collect and organise your information and write, redraft, and proofread the report.

You should write in a formal academic style with simple sentences avoiding slangs and unnecessary jargons. Paragraphs need to be concise and focus on one issue or area of discussion. Tables and diagrams can be used in your report but make sure they add to the reader's understanding of the issues and that they are clearly labelled.

18.5.3 Presentation and Layout: In a report, the content is divided up into a number of sections each with a heading. These sections may be further divided into subsections. Sections and subsections make it easier for the reader to locate the information they need. Normally, these sections and subsections are numbered using a progressive numbering system. Most word processing software will do this numbering for you.

18.5.4 Report Structure:

- **Title:** The title page should have the title of the report, the author's name, and any other details required by the assignment brief such as module/course titles.
- **Contents:** List all the main sections including the appendices remembering to include the page numbers. Any illustrations, tables or diagrams that you have used also need to be included in a separate list in this section.
- **Abstract/Summary:** A brief summary or overview of the report. It should be a document which can be read independently of the main report.
- **Introduction:** A brief description of what the report is about, what it will cover, any relevant background information and any limitations on the contents or coverage of the report.
- **Main Section:** Presents your results to the reader. Depending on the type of report and the instructions you have been given, this section might be further divided into areas such as literature review, methodology, results and discussion.

- **Conclusions:** Summarise the key points from the main body of the report relating them back to the introduction. Do not introduce new material in this section.
- **Recommendations:** This section provides you with the opportunity to suggest changes and improvements. Any recommendations should be based on your conclusions.
- **References:** The reference list should detail all the sources you have used in your report.
- **Appendices:** Use this section to include material that the reader might want to refer to but would disrupt the flow of the main report. Each appendix is numbered so that it can be referred to in the report.

18.6 Writing a Case Study

Most graduate students are unfamiliar with case study and there is often misunderstanding about what a case study is? The case is the "real life" situation and case study is the analysis of that situation. It is an empirical study respected in the academic world and mostly used in the social science research which provides a close, in-depth examination of data within a specific context. In a case study, an individual or individuals, an organization, event, or action in a specific time and geographical location is the subject of the study.

18.6.1 When Should We Use a Case Study Approach?

A case study design is preferred when:

- The focus of the study is to answer "how" and "why" questions.
- When the researcher has little control over events.
- When the focus is on a contemporary phenomenon.
- The boundaries are not clear between the phenomenon and the context.

18.6.2 Key Features of a Case Study:

- It has scientific credentials.
- It is evidence based for professional applications.

18.6.3 Determining the Case for Study: Asking ourselves the following questions can help to determine what our case is:

- Do I want to "analyze" the individual?
- Do I want to "analyze" a programme?
- Do I want to "analyze" the process?
- Do I want to "analyze" the difference between organizations?

18.6.4 Types of Case Studies: Depending upon the purpose of inquiry, there are the following three types of case studies:

- **Intrinsic Case Study:** It is carried out when one wants to gain a deeper understanding of a particular case.
- **Instrumental Case Study:** It is conducted when one has a research question and wants to get insight into the question by studying a particular case.
- **Collective Case Study:** It is the study of a number of cases in order to enquire into a particular phenomenon.

Depending on the type of research question, there are exploratory, descriptive, and explanatory case studies.

- **Exploratory Case Study:** If the research is mainly focused on "what" questions.
- **Explanatory Case Study:** It deals with "how" or "why" questions.
- **Descriptive Case Study:** It focuses on covering the background information and accurate description of the case in question.

Once we have determined that the research question is best answered using a qualitative case study and the case and its boundaries have been determined, then you must consider what type of case study will be conducted. The selection of a specific type of case study design will be guided by the overall study purpose, whether you are looking to describe a case, explore a case, or compare between cases.

18.6.5 Necessary Steps and Elements for Completing the Case Study:

A. Purpose and Rationale for Case Study:

- Significance of the phenomena of interest
- Research questions

B. Design Based on the Unit of Analysis and Research Purpose

C. Data Collection and Management Techniques:

- Field methods
- Transcribed notes and interviews
- Mapping of major concepts
- Building typologies
- Member checking

D. Describe the Full Case

E. Focus the Analysis Built on Themes Linked to Purpose and Unit of Analysis

F. Analyze Findings Based on the Purpose, Rationale, and Research Questions

- Case perspective
- Disciplinary perspective
- Cross-case comparison
- Biography, autobiography, narratives

G. Establishing Rigour

- Credibility
- Transferability
- Dependability
- Conformability

H. Sources: A hallmark of case study research is the use of multiple data sources. Potential data sources may include, but are not limited to:

- Documentation
- Archival records
- Interviews
- Physical artefacts
- Direct observations
- Participant-observation

I. Data Analysis: As in any other qualitative study, the data collection and analysis occur concurrently. The type of analysis engaged in will depend on the type of case study.

18.6.6 How to Write a Case Study: A Sample Format

There are usually eight sections in a case study.

A. Synopsis/Executive Summary:

- Outline the purpose of the case study.
- Describe the field of research—this is usually an overview of the company.
- Outline the issues and findings of the case study without the specific details.
- Identify the theory that will be used.

B. Findings: Identify the problems found in the case. Each analysis of a problem should be supported by facts given in the case together with the relevant theory and course concepts. Here, it is important to search for the underlying problems. This section is often divided into sub-sections, one for each problem.

C. Discussion:

- Summarize the major problem/s.
- Identify alternative solutions to this/these major problem/s (there is likely to be more than one solution per problem).
- Briefly outline each alternative solution and then evaluate it in terms of its advantages and disadvantages.
- No need to refer to theory or coursework here.

D. Conclusion: Sum up the main points from the findings and discussion.

E. Recommendations:

- Choose which of the alternative solutions should be adopted.
- Briefly justify your choice explaining how it will solve the major problem/s .
- This should be written in a forceful style as this section is intended to be persuasive.

F. Implementation:

- Explain what should be done, by whom and by when.
- If appropriate include a rough estimate of costs (both financial and time).

G. References: Make sure all references are cited correctly.

H. Appendices (if any): Note any original data that relates to the study but which would have interrupted the flow of the main body.

19

Explanation of Select Terms Used in Science

Academic language is the language used in textbooks and exams. Academic language differs in structure and vocabulary from language used in daily social interactions. Academic language includes: (i) a *common vocabulary* used in all disciplines, as well as (ii) a *technical vocabulary* inherent to each individual discipline. Academic English is based more upon Latin and Greek roots than is common spoken English. In addition, academic language features more complex language and precise syntax than common English. Low academic language skills are associated with low performance in school.

Science texts contain many specialized terms that may be unfamiliar to students. These terms represent important concepts that are central in understanding science; not knowing such words can impede students' ability to make sense of and learn from informational science texts. While studying science, therefore, students are exposed to new terms that they are unlikely in other subjects, general academic words that have use across the curriculum, and polysemous words for which they know a common meaning, but not the particular meaning used in the science context. The following terms are part of the academic language of science, yet are not specific to science. It is necessary to understand these terms if one is to read and understand science literature:

Acceleration: The rate of change in velocity.

Acid: A substance that produces hydrogen ions in solution; these solutions have a pH less than 7.

Acid Rain: Rain with a pH less than 5.6; produced by substances in the air reacting with rainwater.

Acoustics: The study of sound.

Aerosol: A liquid sprayed from a pressurized container; for example, a can of insect spray.

Alchemist: A medieval version of the modern chemist.

Alcohol: Type of compound formed when -OH groups replace one or more hydrogen atoms in a hydrocarbon.

Allotropes: Different structural forms of the same element.

Alloy: A mixture consisting of a metal and one or more elements.

Allergen: Substance that causes an allergic reaction.

Allergy: Overly strong reaction of the immune system to a foreign substance.

Amalgam: An alloy containing the element mercury; an example is dental fillings.

Amorphous: Something that has no specific shape; for example, a liquid or gas.

Ampere: The unit of measuring current; the rate of flow of electrons in a circuit.

Amplification: The process of increasing the strength of an electric signal.

Antacid: An "anti-acid", or a chemical that changes an acid substance to a neutral substance.

Antibiotics: Chemicals produced by some bacteria that are used to limit the growth of other bacteria.

Antibody: A protein made in response to a specific antigen that can attach to the antigen and cause it to be useless.

Anus: Opening at the end of the digestive tract through which waste leaves the body.

Aqueous: Describes a solution made with water.

Artificial Satellite: Human-made device that orbits Earth.

Artery: Blood vessel that carries blood away from the heart and has thick, elastic walls made of connective tissue and smooth muscle tissue.

Adaptation: Any variation that makes an organism better suited to its environment.

Aerobe: Any organism that uses oxygen for respiration.

Atomic Number: The number of protons in an atom's nucleus.

Balance: A device used in laboratories to measure mass.

Balanced Forces: Forces that are equal in size and opposite in direction.

Base: A substance that produces hydroxide ions (OH-) in solution; these solutions have a pH over 7.

Behaviour: The way in which an organism interacts with other organisms and its environment; can be innate or learned.

Binary Compound: A chemical compound composed of two elements.

Biomass: Organic material from such sources as wood, corn, and wastes from animals and crops.

Bionics: The science of designing artificial replacements for parts of the human body that are not working properly.

Biogenesis: Theory that living things can come only from other living things.

Biosphere: Part of Earth that supports life, including the top portion of Earth's crust, the atmosphere, and all the water on Earth's surface.

Biotic: Features of the environment that are alive or were once alive.

Buoyant force: Ability of a fluid to exert an upward force on an object immersed in the fluid.

Byte: A basic unit of computer memory that represents a character.

Calorimeter: An instrument used to measure changes in thermal energy.

Carbohydrate: An organic compound having twice as many hydrogen atoms as oxygen atoms.

Carnivore: Animal that eats only other animals or the remains of other animals.

Catalyst: A substance that speeds a chemical reaction without itself being permanently changed.

Cell Theory: States that all organisms are made up of one or more cells, the cell is the basic unit of life, and all cells come from other cells.

Ceramic: A material made from dried clay or claylike mixtures.

Chemical Bond: The force that holds together the atoms in a compound.

Chemical Change: The change of substances to different substances.

Chemical Property: A characteristic of a substance that indicates whether it can undergo a specific chemical change.

Chemical Reaction: A change in which one or more substances are converted to different substances.

Chemotherapy: Use of chemicals to destroy cancer cells.

Chyme: Liquid product of digestion.

Combustion: Rapid burning.

Contraction: Movement of molecules toward one another, so that they occupy a smaller space.

Composite: A mixture of two materials, one of which is embedded in the other.

Control: In an experiment, the standard to which the outcome of the test will be compared.

Convex Lenses: Lenses that are thicker in the middle than at the edges; can produce both real and virtual images.

Convex Mirror: A mirror with a surface that curves outward; produces upright, smaller, virtual images of an object.

Corrosive: Hazardous compound that attacks and alters metals, human tissue, or other materials; for example, oven cleaners and battery acid.

Crest: The highest point of a wave.

Crystals: In most solids, the arrangements of particles in repeating geometric patterns.

Conductor: A material that allows electrons to move easily through it.

Condense: To go from the gas state to the liquid state, due to a loss of heat.

Condensation: The change of a substance from a gas to a liquid, which usually takes place when a gas is cooled to or below its boiling point.

Concentration: Generally, the proportion of a solute dissolved in a solvent.

Cyclic Behaviour: Behaviour that occurs in repeated patterns.

Dependent Variable: In an experiment, the factor whose value changes because of a change in the independent variable.

Derived: Unit of measurement obtained by combining SI units.

Diffraction: The bending of waves around a barrier.

Ductile: Ability of metals to be pulled into wires.

Electromagnet: Strong temporary magnet made by inserting an iron core into a wire coil and passing an electric current through the coil.

Ecology: Study of the interactions that take place among organisms and their environments.

Element: Substance in which all the atoms in a sample are alike.

Embryo: Fertilized egg that has attached to the wall of the uterus.

Embryology: Study of embryos and their development.

Energy: The ability to cause change.

Energy Farming: The growing of plants for use as fuel.

Erosion: Movement of soil from one place to another.

Evaporation: The gradual change of a substance from a liquid to a gas at temperatures below the boiling point.

Evolution: Change in inherited characteristics over time.

Experiment: An organized procedure for testing a hypothesis; typically has a control and dependent and independent variables.

Fertilization: In sexual reproduction, the joining of a sperm and egg.

Fetus: A developing baby after the first two months of pregnancy until birth.

Flammable: A chemical characteristic of a substance that allows it to oxidize rapidly.

Fluid: Any material that flows, such as liquids and gases.

Focal Length: The distance from the centre of a lens or mirror to its focal point.

Focal Point: A point on the optical axis of a concave mirror or convex lens where the light rays come together.

Force: A push or pull one body exerts on another.

Frequency: The number of wave crests that pass a point during one second; expressed in hertz.

Friction: The force that opposes motion between two surfaces that are touching each other.

Free Living Organism: Organism that does not depend on another organism for food or a place to live.

Fossil Fuels: Non-renewable energy sources—coal, oil, and natural gas—that formed in Earth's crust over hundreds of millions of years ago.

Fuse: A device that protects an electrical circuit.

Galvanometer: An instrument used to detect electric currents.

Gear: A wheel with teeth around its edge designed to mesh with teeth on another gear so as to transfer force and motion.

Gelatin: A substance obtained by boiling animal bones; used in glues and goods.

Genetics: Study of how traits are inherited through the actions of alleles.

Genus: A group of similar species.

Germination: Series of events that results in the growth of a plant from a seed.

Gestation Period: Period during which the embryo develops in the uterus; the length of time varies among species.

Grounded: Electrically connected to Earth, either directly or through a wire or other metal object.

Habitat: Place where an organism lives and that provides the types of food, shelter, moisture, and temperature needed for survival.

Hacker: A person who uses a computer to break into other computer systems without permission.

Half Life: The amount of time required for one-half of the nuclides in a sample of radioactive isotope to decay.

Hazardous Wastes: Waste materials, such as pesticides and leftover paints that are harmful to human health or poisonous to living organisms.

Heredity: The passing of traits from parent to offspring.

Hertz: The unit of measure for frequency.

Homo Sapiens: Early humans that likely evolved from Cro-Magnons.

Hybrid: An offspring that was given different genetic information for a trait from each parent.

Hydrate: A compound that has water molecules chemically attached to its ions and written into its formula.

Hydraulic: Describes a system operated by the energy of

moving water.

Hypothesis: A testable prediction used to see how something works or to solve a problem.

Incubate: To keep eggs warm until they hatch; the length of time varies among species.

Instinct: Complex pattern of innate behaviour, such as spinning a web that can take weeks to complete.

Independent variable: In an experiment, the factor adjusted to a different value by the experimenter to see what effect it will have on the dependent variable.

Indicator: An organic compound that changes colour in an acidic solution or a basic solution.

Induction: Electrically charging an object or creating an electrical current in it, without physically touching it.

Inertia: The tendency of an object to resist any change in its motion. If motionless, it tends to remain at rest; if moving, it tends to keep moving at the same speed and in the same direction.

Inhibitor: A substance that slows or prohibits a chemical reaction.

Insulator: A material that does not allow heat or electrons to move through it easily.

Internal Combustion Engine: An engine in which fuel is burned inside the engine in chambers.

Ionization: The breaking apart of certain polar substances to form ions when dissolved in water.

Invertebrate: Animal without a backbone.

Joule: The basic unit of energy and work.

Kelvin: The SI unit of temperature.

Kilogram: The SI unit of mass.

Kilowatt Hour: The unit of electrical energy.

Larynx: Airway to which the vocal cords are attached.

Laser: A device that emits a beam of photons that travel in the same direction and phase, producing a beam of coherent light.

Lipids: Fats, oils, and related organic compounds.

Lymphocyte: A type of white blood cell that fights infection.

Magnetic Field: The region around a magnet where magnetic forces act.

Magnifier: A device that makes things appear larger so that more detail can be seen; for example, a microscope.

Medium: A material through which a wave travels.

Metalloids: Elements having properties of both metals and non-metals.

Model: A symbolic representation of an idea, system, or structure to make something understandable.

Modulation: Process of adding voice, music, video, computer information, or other data to radio waves by using electrical currents to vary either amplitude or frequency.

Nearsighted: Describes a person who sees nearby things clearly, but has trouble focusing on distant objects.

Neutralization: A chemical reaction between an acid and a base.

Neutralize: To change an acidic solution or a basic solution so that it is neutral.

Nonelectrolyte: A substance, such as pure water, that does not conduct electricity.

Nuclear Reactor: A device that generates electricity from a controlled nuclear fission chain reaction.

Observation: Using your senses to gather information.

Opaque Materials: Materials you can't see through because they absorb or reflect all light.

Optical Fibre: Transparent glass fibre that can transmit light from one place to another.

Ozone Depletion: Thinning of Earth's ozone layer caused by chlorofluorocarbons (CFCs) leaking into the air and reacting chemically with ozone, breaking the ozone molecules apart.

Physical Change: A change in the size, shape, colour, or state of matter.

Physical Property: Any characteristic material that can be observed without of a changing the identity of the material itself.

Physical Science: The study of matter and energy; topics for study include chemistry and physics.

Pitch: The highness or lowness of a sound, which is determined by the frequency of the sound waves.

Plane Mirror: A mirror with a flat surface that produces a virtual image.

Plasma: A gas like mixture of charged particles that exists at extremely high temperatures.

Pollutant: Substance that contaminates any part of the environment.

Polluted Water: Water that contains high levels of unwanted substances that may be harmful to living things.

Potential Difference: The difference in electric potential energy between two different points; measured in volts.

Potential Energy: Stored energy.

Power: The measure of the amount of work done in a specific amount of time.

Precipitate: An insoluble compound formed during a double-displacement reaction.

Principle: A basic rule or law describing how something always works in the natural world.

Products: In a chemical reaction, the substances produced by the reaction.

Radiation: The transfer of energy in the form of waves. It is a type of energy transfer that does not require matter.

Radio Waves: Electromagnetic waves that have long wavelengths and are used in communications.

Rectifier: Any device that converts alternating current into direct current.

Reflection: Occurs when a wave strikes an object and bounces off.

Refraction: The bending of waves, caused by changing their speed.

Resistance: The opposition to the flow of electrons through a conductor; measured in ohms.

Resonance: The tendency of an object to vibrate at the same frequency as another vibrating source.

Reverberation: The echoing effect produced by multiple reflections of sound.

Semiconductor: An element that conducts electricity under certain conditions.

Solubility: The amount of a substance that will dissolve in a solvent; generally expressed as the maximum number of grams of solute that will dissolve in 100 gm of a solvent at a specific temperature.

Solute: The substance being dissolved in a solvent.

Solution: A homogeneous mixture containing particles so tiny that they cannot be seen even with a microscope.

Solvent: The substance that dissolves a solute.

Standard: In measurement, an exact quantity that everyone agrees to use as a basis of comparison.

State of Matter: Any of the four conditions in which matter can exist: solid, liquid, gas, or plasma.

Sublimation: The process in which a solid changes directly to a vapour without forming a liquid.

Substance: Matter that is an element or a compound.

Symbiosis: Any close relationship between species, including mutualism, commensalism, and parasitism.

Technology: The practical use of scientific information to improve the quality of human life.

Theory: The most logical explanation of why things work the way they do. A former hypothesis that has been tested with repeated experiments and observations and found always to work.

Tidal Energy: Energy produced by the rise and fall of ocean levels; used to generate electricity.

Time: The interval between two events.

Toxic: Hazardous substance that can injure living tissue.

Transistor: A semiconductor that amplifies or strengthens an electrical signal or acts as a tiny off/on switch.

Transmutation: Changing one element to another through radioactive decay.

Trough: The lowest point of a wave.

Ultraviolet Radiation: Electromagnetic waves that have a higher frequency than visible light.

Vaccine: Preparation made from killed bacteria or damaged particles from bacterial cell walls that can prevent some bacterial diseases.

Variable: In an experiment, the one thing that can change.

Vertebrate: Animal with a backbone.

Volt: The unit for measuring electrical potential energy.

Voltage: A difference in electrical potential, measured in volts with a voltmeter.

Water Cycle: Model describing how water moves from Earth's surface to the atmosphere and back to the surface again through evaporation, condensation, and precipitation.

Work: The transfer of energy through motion.

X-ray: Electromagnetic waves having a wavelength shorter than ultraviolet radiation; often used in medical diagnosis and photography because they can penetrate human tissue.

20

Explanation of Select Terms Used in Commerce

The Bachelor of Commerce (B. Com.) Programme expects each student to develop strong written communication skills for a variety of audiences and in a number of business-writing formats. B.Com. students will have the opportunity to write reports, papers, memos, executive summaries and other document styles throughout their academic coursework, and will also create work term reports as part of their co-op work. Effective written communication skills are essential for business professionals, and students will receive performance feedback on their writing from course instructors and co-op staff throughout the programme to support their development.

Acceptance of a Bill: Process by which a buyer (called a drawee) accepts the seller's bill of exchange by signing under the words 'accepted' on face of the bill.

Accommodation Bill: A bill, draft, or note made, drawn, accepted, or endorsed by one person for another without consideration, to enable the second person to obtain credit or raise money.

Adjustment Entries: Entries which are made in the book of account that rectify previous errors.

Ad Valorem: In proportion of the value.

Affidavit: A written declaration upon oath made before an authorized official.

Asset: A single item of ownership having exchange value.

Amalgamation: A consolidation of two or more corporations

B‸d Debts: A debt that cannot be recovered.

Bailment: An act of delivering goods to a bailee for a

particular purpose, without transfer of ownership.

Balance Sheet: A statement of the assets, liabilities, and capital of a business or other organization at a particular point in time.

Bank Reconciliation Statement: A process that explains the difference on a specified date between the bank balance shown in an organization's bank statement, as supplied by the bank, and the corresponding amount shown in the organization's own accounting records.

Bills Payable: It is a document which shows the amount owed for goods or services received on credit.

Bill of Exchange: A written order to a person requiring them to make a specified payment to the signatory or to a named payee; a promissory note.

Bill of Lading: A detailed list of a ship's cargo in the form of a receipt given by the master of the ship to the person consigning the goods.

Bill of Sight: Refers to a declaration made to customs officer by an importer who is unsure about what is being shipped.

Brought Down: Opening balance of a new accounting period, transferred from the previous period.

Brought Forward: Transfers a total sum from the bottom of one page to the top of the next.

Cargo: Goods carried on a ship, aircraft, or motor vehicle.

Carried Down: The balance of an account at the end of an accounting period, which will be taken forward to become the balance at the beginning of a new period.

Carried Forward: Used to refer to an amount at the end of a column, page, or accounting period that is copied at the beginning of the next column, page, or period.

Cash Discount: A deduction allowed by the seller of goods or by the provider of services in order to motivate the customer to pay within a specified time.

Cash on Delivery: The system of paying for goods when they are delivered.

Collateral Security: A property or other asset that a borrower offers as a way for a lender to secure the loan.

Compound Entry: It is an accounting entry in which there is more than one debit, more than one credit, or more than one of both debits and credits.

Consignment Invoice: An export invoice used when goods are sent to someone who is acting for the owner, and who must either sell them or return them to the owner.

Contingent Account: Accounts which are maintained taking into account the contingent events.

Contingent Liability: A potential liability that may occur, depending on the outcome of an uncertain future event. A contingent liability is recorded in the accounting records if the contingency is probable and the amount of the liability can be reasonably estimated.

Counterfoil: The part of a cheque, receipt, ticket, or other document that is torn off and kept as a record by the person issuing it.

Credit: An entry recording a sum received, listed on the right-hand side or column of an account.

Credit Balance: A credit balance on your billing statement is an amount that the card issuer owes you.

Credit Transaction: If the value of a transaction is not met in cash immediately, it is called credit transaction

Credit Note: A receipt given by a shop to a customer who has returned goods, which can be offset against future purchases.

Debit Balance: The ending amount found on the left side of a general ledger account or subsidiary ledger account.

Debit Note: It is a commercial document issued by a buyer to a seller as a means of formally requesting a credit note.

Demurrage: A charge payable to the owner of a chartered ship on failure to load or discharge the ship within the time agreed.

Depreciation: A reduction in the value of an asset over time, due in particular to wear and tear.

Dividend: It is a payment made to shareholders that is proportional to the number of shares owned.

Double Entry System: It means that every business transaction will involve two accounts (or more).

Floating Capital: It denotes currency in circulation and assets which are movable and storable.

Freight: Goods transported in bulk by truck, train, ship, or aircraft.

Gross Profit: Profit a company makes after deducting the costs associated with making and selling its products, or the costs associated with providing its services.

Goodwill: The established reputation of a business regarded as a quantifiable asset and calculated as part of its value when it is sold.

Invoice: A list of goods sent or services provided, with a statement of the sum due for these; a bill.

Insolvent: Unable to pay debts owed.

Instrument: An instrument is a means by which something of value is transferred, held or accomplished.

Investment: The action or process of investing money for profit.

Joint Stock Company: It is a business entity in which shares of the company can be bought and sold by shareholders.

Keelage: A fee charged by certain ports to allow a ship to dock.

Lease: A contract by which one party conveys land, property, services, etc. to another for a specified time, usually in return for a periodic payment.

Ledger: A book or other collection of financial accounts.

Letter of Credit: A letter issued by a bank to another bank (especially one in a different country) to serve as a guarantee for payments made to a specified person under specified conditions.

Liability: A thing for which someone is responsible, especially an amount of money owed.

Limited Company: A private company whose owners are legally responsible for its debts only to the extent of the amount of capital they invested.

Liquidation: Winding up of a firm by selling off its free (unpledged) assets to convert them into cash to pay the firm's unsecured creditors.

Maturity: The time when an insurance policy, security etc. matures.

Memorandum: A document recording the terms of a contract or other legal details.

Merger: A combination of two things, especially companies, into one.

Negotiable Document: It is a document guaranteeing the payment of a specific amount of money, either on demand, or at a set time, with the payer usually named on the document.

Net Profit: The actual profit after working expenses not included in the calculation of gross profit have been paid.

Outstanding Expenses: Those expenses which have been incurred and consumed during an accounting period and are due to be paid, but are not paid.

Partnership: It is a business with multiple owners, each of whom has invested in the business.

Pass Book: A book issued by a bank or building society to an account holder, recording sums deposited and withdrawn.

Paid-up Capital: It is the amount of money a company has received from shareholders in exchange for shares of stock.

Premium: A sum added to an ordinary price or charge.

Prepaid: A current asset representing amounts paid in advance for future expenses.

Profit and Loss Account: This is an income statement prepared to find the net result of a farm.

Quid Pro Quo: A favour or advantage granted in return for something.

Rate of Exchange: Rate at which foreign currencies are exchanged, which may be buying rate or selling rate.

Revenue: Income, especially when of an organization and of a substantial nature.

Securities: Investments that can be traded on a secondary market.

Single Entry: Denoting a system of bookkeeping in which each transaction is entered in one account only.

Speculation: Investment in stocks, property etc. in the hope of gain but with the risk of loss.

Stock-in-Trade: The typical subject or commodity a person, company, or profession uses or deals in.

Stock-Taking: The action or process of recording the amount of stock held by a business.

Subscribed Capital: It is the amount of capital (out of authorized capital) for which company has received applications from the general public who are interested in buying shares.

Suspense Account: This account takes into consideration those entries which do not find a specific book to be posted.

Tariff: A tax or duty to be paid on a particular class of imports or exports.

Trade Balance: It is the calculation of a country's exports minus its imports.

Trade Discount: A discount on the retail price of something allowed or agreed between traders or to a retailer by a wholesaler.

Under Writer: A bank or other financial institution that pledges to buy all the unsold shares in an issue of new shares.

Usance: The time allowed for the payment of foreign bills of exchange, according to law or commercial practice.

Vendor: A person or company offering something for sale, especially a trader in the street.

Voucher: A small printed piece of paper that entitles the holder to a discount, or that may be exchanged for goods or services.

Waiver: A document recording the waiving of a right or claim.

Warranty: A written guarantee, issued to the purchaser of an article by its manufacturer, promising to repair or replace it if necessary within a specified period of time.

Wear and Tear: It is the damage that naturally and inevitably occurs as a result of normal wear or aging.

Working Capital: The capital of a business which is used in its day-to-day trading operations, calculated as the current assets minus the current liabilities.

Working Partner: A partner who takes an active part in the running of a business.

Write off: A cancellation from an account of a bad debt or worthless asset.

Zickri Chits: A letter of protection.

Bibliography

Bailey, Stephen (2011), "Academic Writing: A Handbook for International Students" Third Edition, London: Routledge.

Cooley, L. and J. Lewkowicz (2003), "Dissertation Writing in Practice: Turning Ideas into Text", Hong Kong: The University of Hong Kong Press.

Fulwiler, Toby (2002), "College Writing: A Personal Approach to Academic Writing", Third Edition, Portsmouth: Boynton Publication.

Germano, William (2013), "From Dissertation to Book", Second Edition, Chicago: University of Chicago Press.

Gibaldi, J. (2016), "MLA Handbook for Writers of Research Papers", Seventh Edition. New York: Modern Language Association of America.

Gupta, Renu (2017), "A Course in Academic Writing", Hyderabad: Orient Black Swan.

Hartly, James (2008), "Academic Writing and Publishing: A Practical Handbook", London: Routledge.

Jordan, R.R. (1999), "Academic Writing Course", UK: Longman.

McCarthy, Michael and Felicity O' Dell (1994), "English Vocabulary in Use", London: Cambridge University Press.

Murry, Rowena and Sara Moore (2006), "The Handbook of Academic Writing: A Fresh Approach", Berkshire: UK.

Oshima, Alice (2007), "Writing Academic English", Third Edition, New York: Pearson Longman.

Pak-tao Ng, Pedro (2004), "Effective Writing: A Guide for Social Science Students", Hong Kong: The Chinese University Press.

Reardon, Denis (2006), "Doing Your Undergraduate Project", London: Sage Publications.

Samantray, Kalyani (2015), "Academic and Research Writing: A Course Book for Undergraduate and Research Students", Hyderabad: Orient Black Swan.

Swales, John M. and Christine B. Feak (2012), "Academic Writing for Graduate Students: Essential Tasks and Skills", Third Edition, Ann Arbor: University of Michigan Press.

Swales, John M. and Christine B. Feak (2000), "English in Today's Research World: A Writing Guide", Ann Arbor: University of Michigan Press.

Swan, Michael (2005), "Practical English Usage", Third Edition, Oxford: Oxford University Press.

Wallwork, Adrian (2015), "English for Academic Research: Grammar, Usage and Style", New York: Springer.

Index